WHO WE ARE
vs
WHAT WE ARE

Establishing
A Model of Cooperation
In Our Relationships

WHO WE ARE
vs
WHAT WE ARE

Copyright 2000 by Lorenzo D. Leonard
Printed in the United States of America
All rights reserved
Includes bibliographical references and index
ISBN 0-9660092-6-6
LCC 99-67412

For information about permission to
reproduce selections from this book, write to:
Puget Sound Press
6523 California Ave. SW
PMB292
Seattle, WA 98136-1833
http://www.pugetsoundpress.com
psp@pugetsoundpress.com

Cover design by Dean Ingram
Art work by Lorenzo D. Leonard

1 2 3 4 5 6 7 8 9 0

ALSO BY LORENZO D. LEONARD

RELATIONSHIPS:
Shattering The Lies We Live By!

Abstract Freedom

Made From Scratch by Nella Curatolo
Translated by Lorenzo D. Leonard

WHO WE ARE
vs
WHAT WE ARE

DEDICATION

BIRDS WITH BROKEN WINGS

I have felt compelled for some time now to write about how I have been personally impacted by the legions of birds with broken wings lying heartless along the roadside at the end of their journey, victims of this life's incorrigibility. For the past forty-five years or so, I have witnessed a tragic phenomenon that has consistently played itself out, never once being met with defiance or resistance by the individual who was being adversely influenced by this relentless and unforgiving incorrigibility. For much of my life, I have watched loved ones, friends, and associates leave this mortal life without having soared to the heights of their emotional and spiritual rapture, that is, without having experienced the pinnacle and immeasurable value of who they were innately.

I have watched the last three generations, including my own, pay the ultimate personal price. They have sacrificed a life that was initially set forth in an essence and basic nature that was undeniably good for what, in the end, left them with boundless anguish and grief. I have watched people that I have cared about forgo committing to a personal life

What We Are

that was certain to offer them in return far more than what they were left with as a result of having committed instead to a stifling attachment to mediocrity. The impact, one of self-betrayal, helped to create in these individuals dehumanizing levels of impotent rage, passive-aggressive anger, depression, resentment, and submissive, compliant, and subservient behavior. This is in addition to the assemblage of psychosomatic illnesses that I have also witnessed plaguing these individuals that I have cared so deeply about.

To have emotionally and spiritually soared in their personal lives, the recognition and acknowledgement of the intrinsic value of the qualities and characteristics comprising the undeniable good that each of these individuals embodied would have had to take place. Regretfully so, this simply did not occur. As a result, the lack of mutuality, equality, autonomy, personal legitimacy, joy, and the conviction to live outside of mediocrity in relationships, including the relationship with one's self, became an emotionally and spiritually painful way of life.

When I reexamine my personal history with a focus on the death of my parents, grandparents, aunts, uncles, friends, and close associates, one extremely sad and remorseful reality clutches at my heart. We parted simply as vessels having passed one another at night. We literally had no concept of who the other was internally, only what the

Who We Are

other was externally. Some of the most important and significant people in my life I knew only by what they were rather than who they were: African-American, father, mother, uncle, wife, and postal clerk.

Yes, it is true that on certain occasions, such as birthdays and holidays, I did experience, if only for a fleeting moment, who some of these significant individuals were innately. When my mother, grandfather, uncle, or aunt could feel safe and secure internally to express and display emotional vulnerability, it was then that I could have a quick glance into my human heritage. Such acts of courage allowed me not only to experience their humanity, but encouraged me to be open to experiencing my own as well.

However, this was far more the exception rather than the norm. Experiencing and learning about the qualities and characteristics that comprised who these individuals were innately was virtually an impossible task. <u>This life's relentless incorrigibility, both then and now, is about perfecting what one is externally while playing down the importance of knowing who one is internally.</u> I only know of a few things to be an absolute truth in this life, and the following is certainly one. It is a distinct human tragedy to have shared the privilege of time with a loved one only to be separated by the passing of that individual and to have failed to share with one another

vii

What We Are

those innate qualities and characteristics that represent the embodiment of good inherent in both persons.

<u>When we remove the illusion of importance that accompanies what we are, then we are free to be who we are innately</u>. But this cannot occur until we are ready to accept a personal essence and basic nature that is fundamentally good. Until then, birds with broken wings will continue to line this life's roadside upon completion of one's journey by an incorrigibility that renders heartless its victims.

I dedicate this book to all my loved ones, parents, grandparents, uncles, aunts, friends, and close associates who have passed on in this life before they could heal those broken wings. This book was written to acknowledge to all of these individuals that I have known that their lives were indeed not in vain.

Lorenzo D. Leonard

Contents

Foreword	xi
Preface	1
Introduction	7
Part 1 Understanding The Problem	25
Part 2 Understanding The Solution	77
Conclusion	139
Works Cited	171
Index	173

Puget Sound Press

"*There could be nothing so important
as a book can be.*"
William Maxwell Evarts Perkins (1884-1947)
(Max)

A literary tribute to "the Dean of American editors."

Seattle, Washington

FOREWORD

I was riding on the train from Seattle, Washington to Portland, Oregon this Thanksgiving holiday (1999) thinking about what I would write in the forward to this book. I found myself in somewhat of a "writer's detour" when I was fortuitously enticed into a conversation with a middle-aged African-American man named Royce. He said that he was intrigued by the title of the book that he saw printed at the top of my page of notes, and he proceeded to tell me how he had begun to think about this very same issue some time ago.

At some point in his life, he explained, he became aware of a division within himself, a division between the part that he exhibited to other people and who he really was underneath his exterior. He said that he would mentally prepare for his day before he walked out the door in the morning, determined to see how long he could go saying just what he really thought and felt, before he would revert to showing to others only what they wanted to see and hear. Sadly, he said, he could never go very long before succumbing to the pressure to restrict and stifle his true self. He soon gave up the experiment, feeling frustrated, defeated, and bewildered as to what it was that had beaten and contained him.

What We Are

Royce's experience seemed to capture the problem that so many of us face as we go about our daily routines. We carry with us our hidden passions, thoughts, and feelings that are rendered powerless by fear, guilt, or our need to please others and "get ahead." We are seduced by what our culture says it has to offer us and are willing to give up *who* we really are in order to procure it. After further discussion, Royce and I concluded that to experience true freedom, this would mean experiencing the ability to be and make evident *who* we are in the world regardless of *what* other people expected us to be.

Our serendipitous conversation seemed to reflect the essence of *Who We Are Vs. What We Are*. The author, Lorenzo Leonard, brings to our attention that there is a disquieting dissonance and dis-integrity inside so many of us that is generated by the discrepancy between *who* we really are and *what* we become in the world. But the dissonance, discomfort, and disruption that occurs in the relationships we have with ourselves and others are only the symptoms of the larger core issue, says Mr. Leonard.

The origin of the unnecessary suffering that one may experience is a false belief in one's basic nature; a belief that one is inherently "other than good, bad, or evil." It is this core belief that we hide, defend, and distract from that can drive

Who We Are

and disrupt our lives, our relationships, and ultimately, our society. It is rendered invisible by our compulsion to indulge in the benefits of the "what" world, and the consequences are staggering. It is these beliefs that interfere with our capacity to experience the fullness of relationships and the passions of our hearts, and it seriously compromises the dignity and integrity in our lives. *Who We Are Vs. What We Are* is about acknowledging, sorting through, and confronting our core beliefs in order that we may experience our highest and most noble selves.

Who We Are Vs. What We Are is a gold mine of penetrating thoughts and ideas that offer more than what contemporary psychology has had to offer us to this point. It eloquently presents to us a startling, personal, and hopeful message regarding the value of conflict, the origins of violence and cruelty, and the preservation of integrity in our relationships. It is a message that challenges the reader to take a long hard look in the mirror, but surely promises to enhance and advance a more meaningful way of life. Reading this book leaves one with the warm feeling that Mr. Leonard simply validates what the reader already knew to be true on some level, but had not brought forth into his or her consciousness.

In his book, Mr. Leonard will intimate that you are a good person—innately, undeniably, and unequivocally—not

What We Are

because of *what* you are, but because of *who* you are at your core. The problem, he says, is when we come to depend on and heavily invest in *what we are*—our jobs, wealth, roles, accomplishments, performance, appearance, sexual appeal, athleticism, etc.—in order to prove our worth, justify our existence, maintain our status, or to feel better about ourselves.

We have become so obsessively invested in the end result, that we have been willing, both individually and collectively, to dominate others and sacrifice *who we are* in order to get and stay ahead. In this kind of world, the end justifies the means, no matter how damaging it may be to our integrity. We can create a spiritual and emotional distance within ourselves and in relation to one another that can take us further away from the knowledge that our essence and basic nature is good. In our quest to *feel* good about ourselves, we lose sight of the fact that we *are* good.

The repercussions can be enormous and tragic. As Mr. Leonard writes, "…violence, cruelty, and indifference toward human life is a result of the practice of domination carried out by those who believe their essence to be bad or evil." Consider for a moment the case of Kip Kinkel. He is the young man who killed his parents and later randomly fired his gun into a crowded school cafeteria at Thurston High School in

Who We Are

Springfield, Oregon, in 1998, killing two and wounding twenty-five. Excerpts from Kinkel's personal journal, written prior to the shootings, were read at his sentencing hearing and printed in *The Oregonian* newspaper on November 3, 1999. Portions of the excerpts read as follows:

> "I sit here all alone. I am always alone. I don't know who I am. I want to be something I can never be. I try so hard every day. But in the end, I hate myself for what I've become…I am so consumed with hate all of the time. Could I ever love anyone? I have feelings, but do I have a heart that's not black and full of animosity?…I know that everyone thinks this way sometimes, but I am so full of rage that I feel I could snap at any moment. I think about it every day…There is one kid above all others that I want to kill…The one reason I don't: Hope. That tomorrow will be better. As soon as my hope is gone, people die…Please, someone, help me. All I want is something small. Nothing big. I just want to be happy…I want you to feel this, be this, taste this, kill this. Kill me. Oh God, I don't want to live. Will I see it to the end? What kind of dad would I make? All humans are evil. I just want to end the world of evil. I don't want to see, hear, speak or feel evil, but I can't help it. I am evil. I want to kill and give

What We Are

pain without a cost. And there is no such thing...If there was a God, he wouldn't let me feel the way I do. Love isn't real, only hate remains. Only hate."

Kinkel's journal entries give the public its first real look into his personality, and what we find is a boy who believes himself to be evil and who has projected his belief about himself onto nearly everyone around him. We see an emotionally isolated boy who is consumed with self-hate and a compulsive desire to exact the ultimate act of domination and revenge—to kill those whom he has felt dominated by. His belief that "they" are worthless reflects his belief that *he* is worthless.

As a result, he ultimately did to "them" what he had done to himself (psychically), and his behavior simply validated and reinforced his belief that he was irredeemably evil. He was unable to separate *feeling* bad from *being* bad. And more profoundly, Kinkel was unable to separate from *feeling* evil and *being* evil. In his mind, he *was* what he *did,* and what he did reinforced and reflected his belief that he was evil. Beneath these feelings was no safety net that would have allowed him to feel bad, angry, or rageful and still *know* that his basic nature was good. As Mr. Leonard points out, if one knows that his or her essence and basic nature is innately good, there is no need or inclination to dominate others or strike out in revenge.

Who We Are

We are a nation that on the outside shows its disgust and outrage at the Kip Kinkels of our society. But, well-camouflaged inside, we actually encourage such behavior. We lock up, put away, scapegoat, and demonize "them," and yet continue to invest in developing *what we are* under the influence of the unrecognized belief that we are innately inadequate. We teach our children to hide who they are if it will create conflict, "make" us feel uncomfortable, or jeopardize their performance or advancement in the "what" world.

We compulsively teach our children to bolster their self-esteem to the point that "feeling good" becomes the goal, even if it is at the expense of their emotional integrity. We teach our children that they must be nice and not to say the truth if it means that it will threaten the other person's self-esteem. We protect our children from feeling bad because, in our minds, feeling bad is being bad, and in so doing, we deprive them of the opportunity to learn the difference. We teach our children that they are other than good by obsessively reinforcing and investing in *what* they become rather than in *who* they are. As a nation and as individuals, we have built-in, nearly invisible ways of dominating each other, avoiding conflict, and in the process, creating the conditions for violence, cruelty, and indifference to human life to exist.

As a nation, we are desperately trying to understand how the violence could erupt seemingly out of nowhere in

What We Are

predominantly white, middle-class, suburban environments. Could it be that the Kip Kinkels of our country are simply reflecting back to us *our* sense of powerlessness and *our* desperate attempts to regain our power through punishment, retribution, and control? Witness the increased popularity of the death sentence and mandatory prison terms for convicted criminals. Witness the extraordinary security measures implemented in so many of our nation's middle and high schools.

Witness laws that, in effect, mandate a double punishment for hate crimes. These statements attest to Americans' resolve to not tolerate such wanton disregard for human life. But beneath our bravado and reflected in our reaction to the violence are the signs of a fearful and impotent people grasping desperately to regain control. We exhibit virtually the same response to conflict—threats and demonstration of power, retribution, and domination—that characterizes the reaction of these young killers. Who is reacting to whom?

The focus and obsession on *what* we are contributes greatly to the objectification and subordination of women as well. One of the saddest aspects of this reality is the number of women who continue to internalize and hang on to a belief in their innate inadequacy and inferiority. We see the psychologically destructive effects of such a belief when women are submissive to men and dependent upon them for approval,

Who We Are

when they dress and act in such a way as to draw and secure the attention and admiration of men, or when they reactively strive to achieve success and status—all at the expense of *who* they really are.

To reinforce this assertion, I draw upon the comments of Leslie Jane Seymour, editor-in-chief of *Redbook* magazine (as reported in *The Oregonian* newspaper on November 1, 1999). Her magazine (as well as a host of others) admittedly emphasizes how women can best manipulate men in order to entice them into relationships or how they can hang on to them once they've "got 'em." "Women say they don't like it when we write about how to please your man…(they say) what about how to please themselves or a man making an effort? But every time we write about that, it bombs," says Ms. Seymour. "And every time we write about how to please your man, it sells. <u>Magazines are a business, and my job is to give a woman what she's really interested in, not what she thinks she's supposed to say she's interested in.</u>"

A convenient example of the demeaning objectification and subjugation encouraged by a popular women's magazine is found in the December 1999 issue of *Cosmopolitan*. The featured articles listed on the cover include the following:

Cosmo Sex School:
Study Up on Seduction
Learn New Tricks With Your Lips

What We Are

*Earn an A+ Under the Covers
Now Go to the Head of <u>His</u> Class*

*Be the Girl Every Guy Wants:
7 Tiny Tricks That Make Men Melt
(We Tell You <u>Exactly</u> What They Are)*

*The World's 8 Sexiest Models:
They've Got the Lips, the Eyes, the Hair, and the Bods
That Are Oh-So Cosmo*

*Love Coupons (Just for Him):
These Bedroom Passes Will Leave Him Breathless*

Cosmopolitan is one of the best-selling magazines that cater to women, and it has been for some time. It is bought almost exclusively by heterosexual women. Certainly, every woman has the right to choose which magazine she buys, and clearly, men and women have a right to profit from the sale of this magazine. Those who vociferously support one's right to buy or sell this type of magazine have no quarrel with me. <u>I simply find that the popularity of this type of magazine, with the focus on demeaning, dehumanizing manipulation, to be reflective and exploitive of women who believe themselves to be flawed, inadequate, and valued less than men.</u> In my mind, this type of magazine distorts femininity, does little to advance or enhance the resilience and strength of women, and in fact helps to perpetuate their domination and false beliefs about themselves. The existence and popularity of

Who We Are

these magazines mirrors back to us the pervasiveness of the internalized belief (in men and women) that woman is innately inadequate and in need of a man to "complete" her.

Kip Kinkel's violence and the internalized domination experienced by so many women, are but two examples of the potentially destructive and divisive impact that our core beliefs can have in our lives and in the lives of others. Mr. Leonard offers us a vision of a more fulfilling way of life founded on emotional integrity, accountability, and compassion. He reminds us that an intimate and respectful relationship with someone else begins with learning to accept and embrace our own essence and basic nature as undeniably good. In order to realize our higher selves, we must begin to shed that which dominates us and let go of our investment in that which is superficial and unimportant. We learn that our endeavor to enhance one another enhances ourselves and opens the doors to a more meaningful way to relate to one another. Mr. Leonard's vision is a lofty one, but is securely grounded in empathy, dignity, mutual respect, and unconditional love.

To date, the professional recommendations and popular solutions to our deteriorating relationships have offered us little more than better ways to adapt, adjust, react to, and control the ever more volatile *symptoms* that we are witnessing. In contrast, *Who We Are Vs. What We Are* exposes and treats the *underlying disease* at its source. It is a vision that

What We Are

runs counter to the immediate-gratification, self-indulgent, and symptom-focused culture that we seem to have created and it challenges us to reconstruct our notion of what the American dream really is.

If we are to adequately address the seemingly senseless and heretofore unimaginable acts of violence, if we are to break the cycle of female objectification and male entitlement, if we are to raise our children to preserve each other's dignity, if we are to increase the value of integrity and accountability in our relationships, and if we are to learn from and give meaning to our past conflicts, then we must listen carefully to what Lorenzo Leonard has to say. The road to our enhancement and advancement begins with awareness and accountability for our actions. *Who We Are Vs. What We Are* helps us take the first step in this direction and promises a more meaningful, compassionate, and fulfilling existence in return.

For Royce, and all those like him who are seeking the freedom and support to develop and nurture *who* they are, I cannot think of a better book to recommend.

Steve Russell
author of *BEING NICE AT A PRICE:*
Emotional Domination, Depression,
and the Search for Autonomy

Who We Are

PREFACE

The most difficult and painful challenge that I continue to face on a daily basis is the acknowledgement and acceptance that *who* I am innately is undeniably good. Good as opposed to inherently defective, flawed, corrupt, bad, evil, or something other than good, which would include not equal to, inadequate, less than, and not enough. To concede that I am the embodiment of good has been one of my deepest sources of grief. Good with respect to compassion and love without prerequisites, support and encouragement without selfish motives, and a single-mindedness to protect the dignity of other individuals as well as myself. Those individuals that have directly experienced my less-than-good behavior are another source of grief for me.

What We Are

To finally acknowledge and accept my personal responsibility to promote this same truth for my family, community, and society is yet one more chamber of grief for me. Emotionally and spiritually separating from a self-perception, which has haunted me throughout my life, that I was less than good has not been an easy task to overcome. Not equal to, less than, and not enough have created ample wreckage in my life to last two lifetimes. I also continue to face the painful challenge of maintaining a commitment and conviction to honor the inherent good of individuals who have injured me emotionally, psychologically, and physically. There have been numerous occasions when I have consciously or unconsciously conspired to make this a reality. And there have been numerous occasions when I have not participated in my personal coup d'état.

Be that as it may, the inherent and undeniable good of those individuals requires acknowledgement and acceptance on my part. If I am to live with a conviction that my inherent good is now the foundation for *who* I am, then the inherent good of another individual requires that recognition as well. Despite a history of hurtful behavior between us, this truth still requires recognition and acceptance by me. When I reexamine past experiences that resulted in injury either to others or to myself, I witness contemptible

Who We Are

behavior that perpetuated personal indignity. In contrast to those unfortunate moments, the pursuit of experiences resulting in its opposite are now a priority in my life.

In the midst of wrestling with acknowledging and accepting that I am a good person, I often feel unsteady. I have come to realize that this feeling is closely associated with my personal responsibility to uphold the dignity, integrity, and autonomy of my family, community, and society. My fear and insecurity regarding this personal responsibility is that I will not know the true identity of an individual, or even myself, when I am visited with internal or external conflict.

I feel afraid and anxious that a truth which encapsulates all of us, individually and collectively, will be set aside in favor of a lie that supports a belief that another individual and myself are indeed less than good. Conflict does have the capability to instigate a temporary forgetfulness, abandonment, and self-betrayal if one is not anchored in his or her inherent and undeniable good. And yet, I realize that it is the presence of conflict—an indispensable vehicle—that will transport me to an emotional and spiritual acceptance that those comprising my human community, including myself, are innately and undeniably good.

What We Are

Conflict is a teacher, not the adversary I once believed it to be. Once I can accept without hesitation and reservation that I am the guardian of another individual's dignity, integrity, and autonomy, as well as for myself, I can truly participate in this life from a position of honest intentions. No longer will hidden agendas and coercion be considered necessary instruments to move me from one point to another. The exhibitionism of *what* I am and the consistent feeling that I am less than good can no longer out distance the truth of *who* I am. Compassion and sensitivity to the needs of others, as well as support and encouragement to experience one's dignity, replaces the pageantry that *what* I am is prone to produce.

If the above mentioned personal challenges seem like a tall order, then I would certainly be in agreement. If the above mentioned personal challenges seem humanly impossible to achieve in one's lifetime, then I would heartily disagree. There is no question that to redirect my attention and effort to exercising *who* I am in my life, which is in direct opposition to *what* I am, is a significant endeavor. However, if I can devote incredible amounts of energy and time to support a way of life based on *what* I am, then I can work toward a goal that I know will leave me with some measure of self-dignity and self-respect. A way of

Who We Are

life primarily based on *what* I am in the end provides me with conspicuous disappointment and shame. "I want to look good so that I feel good" is a mentality that I am ready to immediately discard. This type of thinking causes far too many problems that are personally unfulfilling and unsatisfying, among other things.

I have written this book to expose the mental anguish and emotional despair that occurs for an individual who attempts to live with *who* he or she is innately while in conflict with *what* he or she is externally. Solutions to remedy this mental anguish and emotional desperation are also included in this book. Good versus nice, domination versus cooperation, and abstract freedom versus real freedom are the personal conflicts facing us all, both individually and collectively. The task is quite simple to understand; it is the execution of the task that is complex and difficult to put into action. Living one's life from a place of personal commitment and sacrifice in order to protect the dignity, integrity, and autonomy of another person, as well as one's self, requires that an individual acknowledge and accept his or her personage as inherently and undeniably good. This goal is certainly achievable within one's lifetime.

What We Are

*words
matter:
write to learn
what you know.*

Mary Anne R. Hersey

INTRODUCTION

What We Are

On August 1, 1980, I began my career as an alcohol and drug counselor at a small hospital on Chicago's West Side. This change of profession seemed like a natural one to make at this time in my life. After graduating from college, I had spent seven pain-filled years in and out of blackouts and drunkenness. And I was high on every imaginable drug that could be purchased both over and under the counter. It never mattered that I was mixing alcohol and drugs; the combination of the two was desperately needed to help ease the emotional and spiritual pain I was in, or so I thought.

The profession that I was minimally involved in for those seven years was as an accountant and auditor. I remember feeling emotionally isolated and cut-off from people while working in this profession of schedule A and B, explicit standards, and endless numbers. And what seemed to intensify my life at this time was the strong desire to liberate people from more than just the burden of their inflated income and taxes. So, why not attempt the journey to save others from the living hell that these two seductive addictions create for those in need of tunneling downward into a belief that his or her essence and basic nature is bad? This is the reason why an individual would seek an up-close and personal relationship with addictions of this nature.

Who We Are

During this period of time, I embraced and accepted the belief that my essence and basic nature was *bad*. In otherwords, I believed that I was morally and spiritually a *bad* person. Accepting the position as an alcohol and drug counselor was a great way to avoid taking personal responsibility to transition out of this lie. I did not begin my life with this deep-seated feeling of being flawed and *bad*, but I certainly was married to this lie at this period in my life with a perverted sense of loyalty.

My early experiences as a young boy and adolescent had taught me to believe that my essence and basic nature was *something other than good*. And by *something other than good*, I mean feeling less than, not equal to, inadequate, and not enough. All that I needed to set me on the downward spiral to feeling *bad* about myself were experiences that reinforced this particular belief. Tragically speaking, the diseases of alcoholism and drug addiction provided me with such experiences.

There were extenuating circumstances that supported my belief that I was at least borderline qualified to be an alcohol and drug counselor. I had completed two alcohol and drug treatment programs, and I knew the experience of relapse extremely well. I had just traveled down this

What We Are

heart-breaking and family-crushing road with these addictions, and I was aware of some of the self-inflicted wounds. For instance, the pervasive and powerful denial system for alcoholism. I knew all too well that alcoholism is a disease that will soundly attempt to convince the alcoholic that he or she does not have a drinking problem. Hence, what better candidate than myself to take on the task of saving an individual from his or her living hell brought on by the addiction to alcohol and drugs?

I remember thinking to myself that if I could take care of and save an individual from his or her personal torment with continued drinking or drug use, then I could feel good about myself. I would not have to be reminded of the personal crisis that I was still living with inside of myself. The equation that I developed for myself was simple. If I worked hard enough to convince a substantial number of clients to stay in recovery, then I could possibly reverse the inner belief that I was a *bad* person. This had to be the answer: the more people I could save, the more successful I would be at redeeming my sense of feeling defective. As I relive this period of time in my life, I can remember how a large part of my personal living hell had to do with desperately wanting to be released from my

Who We Are

emotional and spiritual acceptance that my essence and basic nature was *bad*.

From the time that I was a little boy, I had always believed that I was basically a good person. My innocence, creativity, sense of community, adventure, and passion felt right and solid. However, to my disadvantage, I lacked the personal experiences of being able to live my life based on *who* I was innately. This type of experience growing up would have allowed me to learn that I was basically *good* because I would have had this embodiment of good mirrored back to me by the adults in my life. And though I had always believed that I was a good person, what made this even more difficult to accept was the fact that I had no real clue as to *who* I was on this innate level. Understanding that I was a good person on an intuitive and intellectual level was not enough to help transition me out of this negative self-perception.

I actually worked six years, three years in Chicago and three years in Portland, Oregon, as an alcohol and drug counselor. My superiors and peers at both treatment facilities were continuously impressed with my ability to give dynamic lectures, maintain meticulous staffing notes,

What We Are

counsel, motivate, and interact with clients. I worked extremely hard and compulsively to create a larger-than-life reputation for myself based on *what* I was: an alcohol and drug counselor that you did not want to lock horns with on any given workday.

I literally had nothing else to draw on from within myself, so I was compulsively driven most of the time to fulfil this role that I felt compelled to create for myself. The more effort I put into *what* I was, the more I could distract from the emotional and spiritual pain that I was so frantically trying to ignore. My life during this period of time had been strictly constructed around *what* I was and completely devoid of any input that emanated from *who* I was.

There are individuals who have stated to me that this last statement is incorrect. Each has said that there were numerous instances when they did experience *who* I was and the good that I embodied. And this was evidenced by my love and genuine concern for people, a strong sense of community, compassion, and understanding with respect to the hardships created by alcoholism and drug addiction. However, after receiving this information, I have often felt compelled to tell the truth about the motivation behind the behavior they observed as good.

Who We Are

It was difficult at first to be honest about my intent, but the more I could accept my emotional and spiritual state of deficiency, the more I was able to be accountable for my actions. Though I could be observed demonstrating these behaviors, the assumption cannot be made that these behaviors were emanating from a legitimate place, such as *who* I was innately. To the contrary, these behaviors were emanating from a false place, and were part of an unhealthy agenda designed to distract people from what I was really feeling about myself.

Internally, I was struggling with the belief that my essence and basic nature was *bad*. Therefore, what people observed about my external behavior was nothing more than a façade. Being nice and acting good became a useful social cover to conceal a self-image, which if exposed to other people, I felt I would be horribly rejected for and not liked. It was very important that people like me and find me socially acceptable. Doing what other people wanted me to do became a way of life. And it was much easier to look and act good, rather than to take time out of my life to learn to know that I was good. Besides, this process would be too costly with respect to the pain and money that would be involved, or so I thought.

What We Are

Needless to say, I eventually crashed and burned emotionally, psychologically, and spiritually. The eventual breakthrough came in stages, with the first being that I would transition out of a self-perception of being a *bad* person into one that I was *something other than good*. I am truly grateful that I have never believed myself to be an *evil* person. Though it is not impossible to transition out of this self-perception, the work that is required to do so is extremely intense and difficult. The events that instigated moving from one belief to another were a series of failed relationships, and the suffering that I helped to create in the lives of people around me. I had found a way to emotionally and spiritually hide out in the helping profession, but not without a cost to those that I was enlisted to help, to my loved ones, and mostly to myself.

One fact is for certain: in the helping profession the trained specialist cannot take a client or patient emotionally and spiritually to a place where he or she has not personally resided. Yes, the attempt is vigorously made, but to no avail. If the professional cannot insert *who* he or she is innately into the work that is being performed, then the work itself will eventually become unsatisfying to both the client or patient and the professional. And *who* the professional is on an innate level is the embodiment of good and those qualities that comprise this good.

Who We Are

The client or patient has to be seen in the same light, if the work is to be effective. Compassion, sensitivity, and autonomy will be experienced as genuine by the client or patient if the trained specialist has incorporated these qualities into his or her life. If this important aspect of living from an authentic place is ignored, then the results are surely to indicate a lack of depth. Presuming this is the case, then all that the professional is doing is merely teaching a client or patient to adapt and adjust to the emotions that are dominating this individual.

Hopefully, the professional is committed to teaching and assisting the client or patient to identify and disengage from internalized beliefs that are provoking him or her to manifest behavior that is insulting and degrading to others as well as to oneself. The most commonly held negative self-perceptions that I have experienced both personally and professionally are believing that one is either *something other than good*, *bad*, or *evil*.

And some of the more popular recommendations for helping a client or patient to adapt and adjust to the presence of conflict are affirmations, different vitamins, change the exercise program, or take a vacation. These recommendations do not move the client or patient to the core

What We Are

issue. They are designed to help a client or patient *feel* good, rather than to know that he or she is *innately* good. Conflict is unavoidable, and hopefully it will be viewed as a teacher. But more importantly, if the presence of conflict produces condemnation, unkind judgement, cruelty, or violence then what is being unmasked is a tightly held internal belief about one's self that is an emphatic lie.

Accepting the truth about myself was not an easy position to embrace, especially after living a lie for so many years. To know that *who* I am is the embodiment of good on an emotional and spiritual level, and to be able to identify those qualities that I embody that are undeniably good was excruciatingly painful. It still is, but to a much lesser degree. For over twelve years, I have been counseling people in my private practice. The six years that I worked as an alcohol and drug counselor, plus twelve years in private practice, and my personal emotional and spiritual work has taught me one irrefutable fact. It is the inner acceptance, by an individual, of a personal essence and basic nature that is either *something other than good, bad*, or *evil* is what produces condemnation, insensitive judgement, cruelty, and violence.

It matters not what race, color, religion, or class a person may represent. What I have observed over eighteen

Who We Are

years in the counseling profession are individuals seeking emotional, physical, and spiritual relief from the presence of conflict in either their personal or interpersonal relationships. Personal relationships include the individual, and interpersonal relationships include work and recreational relationships. What I have learned over this period of time is that the source of an individual's external and internal conflict is primarily a result of having embraced a self-perception that is less than good.

And since conflict, in our society, is seen as an adversary rather than as a teacher, condemnation, insensitive judgement, cruelty, and violence are behaviors customarily used to resolve the conflict. I have observed parents and their children, husbands and wives, lovers, siblings, and long-standing friends emotionally, physically, and spiritually brutalize one another in reaction to the presence of conflict as it pertained to their relationship. Unfortunately, the purpose or intent of this behavior was to dominate and gain some measure of control over the other.

A majority of clients that I have worked with over the years have personally struggled with a self-perception that he or she is *something other than good*. Again, by

What We Are

something other than good, I mean internally feeling less than, not equal to, inadequate, and not enough. I have worked with a significant number of clients who have struggled internally with an essence and basic nature believed to be *bad*. And I can only recall working with two or three clients during this time frame who believed that his or her essence and basic nature was *evil*. It has been my experience that this particular individual usually will not seek counseling due to a pervasive sense of hopelessness. I have used the phrase, *struggled with a self-perception that he or she is something other than good* because when the issue of conflict was further explored during counseling this became evident as the core issue.

My particular focus in working with clients in the counseling profession has been in the area of relationships, including the relationship with oneself. In our society, we expend very little time and effort focusing on the merits of *who* an individual is innately. As a result of this lack of focus, the personal characteristics that would comprise *who* an individual is innately and the good that these characteristics embody remain undeveloped.

Therefore, a great deal of emphasis is placed on *what* an individual is, and here is where the practice of domination is given credibility by becoming a formidable way of life. A way of life that is based on *what* an individual is sets the stage for unethical and corrupt competition, which is a major principle whereby domination is established. The playing field of opportunity is never equal for those individuals in positions to be dominated.

The basis for indignity and disrespect, which includes violence, cruelty, and condemnation, is the practice of domination. The irresistible need to exert power and control over another individual, including one's self, is the influencing factor that propels the practice of domination. And the basis for the practice of domination is the belief that one's personal essence and basic nature is less than good. We simply are not educated nor encouraged to accept the good that we embody, both individually and collectively. If this were true, then there would be no need to dominate one another or one's self with such behavior.

The fact of the matter is that the practice of domination is all around us. The very organ that produces a genuine and morally legitimate existence in an individual is not recognized and given credibility, that is, the innate good that each individual embodies. Compassion, sensitivity, community, love that knows no prerequisite, creativity,

What We Are

adventure, passion, and genius are just a few of the qualities that comprise the innate good of an individual. This is *who* an individual is regardless of what he or she may outwardly represent. *Who* an individual is internally will always stand opposed to *what* he or she is externally, unless the internal is allowed to be the external garment worn by that individual. *What* an individual is simply cannot sustain and preserve life; it is simply a way of life based on the absence of a formidable good.

Our parents, grandparents, great-grandparents, and great-great-grandparents contributed enormously to the incredible standard of living that has been achieved in our country to date. European, Native, African, Hispanic, and Asian Americans have contributed heavily to the economic and social development that has made American society one that is envied throughout the world. Those that came before us took extreme care to develop a way of life that is primarily fixated with the external element of an individual's life. Because they were extremely busy and preoccupied with sculpting out this vast material wealth we have at our disposal, they were unable to focus much attention on the spiritual and emotional component to an individual's life.

Who We Are

Sure, our ancestors had religion, which helped to endure the rigors of sculpting out a way of life. Despite what side of town or the tracks a person was decreed legitimate or otherwise, religion offered some emotional and spiritual relief. Nonetheless, what our ancestors lacked was a true sense of spirituality. What they lacked was a spirituality that could be demonstrated as an active commitment to be the guardian of the dignity, integrity, and autonomy of another human being as well as to one's self. This naturally could only come later in the development of our society after the business of setting up shop was completed.

The challenge to develop emotional and spiritual skills that will elevate us, both individually and collectively, to a more sophisticated and mature self-perception stands before us as the next frontier to explore. Acting from the aged script of *what* we are has now become an obsolete way of life. This way of life has served its purpose; it has moved us to this stage in our growth as a society. It has now become necessary to focus on developing another valuable aspect to our existence, and that explicitly is *who* we are innately.

To recognize and accept that *who* we are individually is the embodiment of good will naturally propel us to elevate

What We Are

our individual self-perceptions. What this will immediately accomplish is rendering archaic the need to practice domination in our primary and secondary relationships. In its place is the practice of cooperation, because there simply is no necessity to compete for power and control over another individual or one's self. Also, what this will immediately accomplish is rendering archaic the notion that an individual is *something less than good* if he or she cannot measure up to standards based on external circumstances.

Just as important, developing the emotional and spiritual skills that will create a more sophisticated and mature self-perception will also be the most effective deterrent to insensitive judgement, cruelty, and violence. An individual who has been taught that he or she is the embodiment of good will seek to promote the inherent good of another individual, as well as continue to develop and enhance the inherent good of one's self. Merging this emotional and spiritual way of life into our well-established material and technological life can provide the balance that our society seems in search of today. This, I believe, is what summons our individual and collective attention as we transition into the twenty-first century.

Until such time, my clients and I will continue to struggle with the following questions: Why is it that a person

Who We Are

would rather believe that he or she is less than good instead of knowing that he or she is good? Why is it that we, individually and as a society, will spend incredible sums of money and time to *feel* good, but will actively resist investing the equivalent to know that we, individually, *are* good? Lastly, why is it that we, as a society, will profess to be good, but will permit and allow another human being to be treated as though he or she is less than good? I truly suspect that the answers to these questions will remain nebulous, so long as *who* we are is in conflict with *what* we are.

What We Are

What is it that I know to be true that would be based on the wisdom extracted from my personal experiences? If it were autonomy, emotional integrity, personal legitimacy, and dignity that an individual would seek to experience in his or her relationships, in otherwords a personal freedom, then the illusions that once promised and supported a pseudo state of emancipation would necessarily be discarded.

Only those individuals in compliance with a position of weakness and timidity seek to maintain illusions that provide a social cover suggesting control, independence and self-determination. And of course, the quest for personal freedom for once and for all is settled when the issue of an essence and basic nature is successfully negotiated under the terms of an undeniable good.

Lorenzo D. Leonard

PART 1
UNDERSTANDING THE PROBLEM

What We Are

*If relationships are to work and be meaningful,
then we, who comprise the American society,
will fittingly accept that we are the guardians of
one another's dignity, autonomy, and respect.
We have no other recourse than to put this way
of life into an active format if we, as a society, are to
persist as a cohesive nation with diverse
cultures and ethnicity during the twenty-first century.*

Lorenzo D. Leonard

On the front page of *The Seattle Times* newspaper, dated May 2, 1999, one headline read: "How can we know our schools are safe?" The headline and its corresponding story were written in response to the deadly shooting sprees that occurred at Columbine High School in Littleton, Colorado in April, as well as at other high schools throughout our nation during the past six years. My immediate thought in response to the question was that the answer was all too apparent and uncomplicated. I recall stating out loud, "The answer to this question requires very little thought if one is willing to have the courage and emotional integrity to respond to it with honesty."

Our schools, both public and private, will be safe from the mounting carnage, senseless acts of violence, and cruelty when American society is safe. And our society will be safe when we have the courage to put into daily practice a model of cooperation, one that favors personal accountability. The model of domination that we historically and currently use, and one which sadly rules out personal accountability, can then be dismantled.

This particular model has been far too destructive, intensely dividing our society with respect to sexism, racism, classism, and homophobia. Personal and interpersonal relationships have suffered as well, because the presence of internal and external conflict is viewed as an adversary rather than as a teacher. Methods of resolution are often hurtful and harmful when reacting to conflict in this manner. Unfortunately, the practice of domination is a method that is used more often than not to resolve internal and external conflict in our society.

Since its inception, American society, to no one's surprise, has established a way of life primarily based on

What We Are

the practice of domination. Our young history as a nation is replete with the practices of domination being brought to bear against every ethnic and cultural group comprising our society. The various forms in which the practice of domination can be evidenced are emotional, psychological, spiritual, sexual, physical, political, legal, and economic. It is a practice that can be applied against one's self, as well as against others. Domination actually exemplifies a model of weakness, one that is perpetuated through fear, intimidation, and force. The intent of this behavior is to achieve power and control rather than mutuality, emotional integrity, and personal dignity.

Historically, our society has held an expectation that each generation of children practice in their relationships a congeniality and harmony with respect to gender, race, and religious differences. And this expectation applies as well to when our children are experiencing other forms of conflict that are personal in nature. For example, when feeling anxious, inadequate, confused, and lonely we expect our children to show some restraint and behave as miniature adults. This expectation has been maintained throughout our history as a society in spite of the obvious. And the obvious is that we, the adults, have been unwilling to practice congeniality, harmony, and restraint when we

Who We Are

are faced with the identical differences and conflicts as our children.

The manner in which we resolve gender, race, political, economic, and religious differences in our society is through the use of domination, avoidance, and blame. Other forms of conflict that transpire in personal or interpersonal relationships reveal the same pattern as well. For example, road rage, which is a new and different form of emotional domination, has emerged recently and is gaining nationwide concern. While driving on our highways, expressways, and freeways, more and more motorists are reacting to external conflict by using their automobiles as a dangerous weapon. This type of behavior and others like it is reactionary to the presence of conflict, and it is totally opposite the expectation that we have of our children.

Our children observe that we, the adults, use condemnation, cruelty, and violence to gain power and control over others or one's self as a means to resolving personal and interpersonal conflicts. They keenly observe that we, the adults, lash out with violence and cruelty against others or one's self when we perceive either rejection or are not satisfied with the results of our personal agendas. As a society, we have failed to model for our children a way of

What We Are

life that teaches them through example how to be supportive and protective, first of one's own dignity, respect, and integrity, and secondly of another individual's. Yet there is a strong tendency on the part of many adults in our society to wash their hands of any responsibility for the mounting carnage, violence, and cruelty acted out by our children. What I know to be true is this: "the apple does not fall far from the tree." Our collective focus has been and continues to be on the apple (the child), and little if any genuine attention is ever focused on the tree (the adult).

Because relationships are primarily exposed to the practice of domination rather than a model of cooperation, it is a difficult challenge to put into practice a truism that involves each individual comprising our society. That truism is as follows: whether accepted or not, the fact remains that we, individually and collectively, are the guardians of one another's dignity, autonomy, and respect. We share a commonality, a familiarity with one another that links us together regardless of gender, class, race, or religious beliefs. We are representatives of a humanity that carries with it a personal responsibility to protect and advance all of its cultures.

Let us not forget that children are primarily emotional mirrors that will reflect back to us what they experience

Who We Are

being modeled in front of them. With this in mind, it makes perfect sense that we would continue to experience from our children an increase in violence, cruelty, and self-destruction if we, the adults, continue to expose them to a way of life that is based on domination. We cannot expect them to use a model of cooperation when conflict occurs in their relationships while they observe adults continuing to use a model of domination to resolve conflict.

The adult sports enthusiast can be overheard preaching to the young and impressionable athlete entering the sophisticated world of sports, "In order to win, we must dominate our opponent…but don't forget, we also must have teamwork in order to accomplish this feat!" We teach and perpetuate the appropriateness of domination by insisting that to win at all costs is a true sign of team dedication and conviction. The end result is given priority rather than the development of an individual's character.

Through competitiveness that is adversarial in nature and supportive of establishing one-up-one-down relationships, the practice of domination in the circle of sports is encouraged. We teach the model of domination relative to our opponent, but expect the model of cooperation to

What We Are

be adhered to relative to the community or team. We cannot have it both ways. We encourage humility, but teach arrogance, which is a breeding ground for privilege and entitlement. We invite our children to strive for power and control over others and self rather than mutuality and personal dignity.

What a confusing experience for a child to be exposed to at such a young age! This approach ignores the recognition, acceptance, and nurturing of the absolute good, which is the essence and basic nature of a child. To teach a more accurate portrayal that sports is truly about developing the innate characteristics of a child seems more suitable to his or her emotional and spiritual growth. Emphasizing the importance of developing character, discipline, sense of community, and that an opponent is deserving of respect as well as one's self reinforces the absolute good in a child. When we, as adults, underscore the importance of *what* a child is rather than *who* the child is innately, the opportunity to have mirrored back to him or her the innate good is greatly hampered.

Davey Johnson, the Los Angeles Dodgers manager, was quoted in *The Oregonian*, a Portland newspaper on December 14, 1998, making a statement that offers

Who We Are

clarification about the American way relative to the practice of domination. After successfully signing pitcher Kevin Brown to a preposterous $105 million contract, Johnson offered this explanation to justify the acquisition, which was made possible because of the deep financial pockets of the Dodgers. Manager Johnson stated, "Parity is not the American way. The American way is to dominate somebody else."

Unfortunately, this troubling message, which justifies the practice of domination, is preached daily to our children, both in and out of the sports arena. One can only imagine how confusing this must be for a child to hear, especially when he or she is also taught that cooperation is an essential component to being successful. The practice of domination eliminates the possibility of experiencing relationships that are based on equality, emotional integrity, and dignity. Power and control do not generate relationships that are intimate and mutual. Fear, envy, resentment, and disrespect are the atmosphere that is generated between individuals who construct a relationship that is governed by domination.

What precisely is domination and how is it that we are so driven to make this a practice in our relationships

What We Are

when we consistently experience that the end results are inequality and contempt? Steven Russell in his book, *Being Nice at A Price: Emotional Domination, Depression, and the Search for Autonomy*, defined emotional domination as, "a state of pervasive, yet often invisible, suppression of natural emotions, thoughts, and actions." I would add "conflict that arises in relationships with self and others due to the practice of domination occurs because there is either covert or overt behavior that limits or restricts a natural flow of feelings, thoughts, or actions."

For instance, a wife may experience inner turmoil as a result of feeling unseen and unheard with respect to being excluded from decisions that affect the marriage as a whole. She wants to experience more equality in the marriage. Specifically, she wants to have input about when and where to buy a new family home, where to take the family vacation, and what family vehicle to purchase. After being accountable by telling her husband how she feels emotionally impacted by being excluded from decision-making experiences, her husband reacts with either anger or rage and attempts to shame his wife.

He seeks to maintain emotional and economical domination over his wife by devaluing and taking a position of opposition with regard to what she is feeling. The husband also makes a concerted effort to diminish her base of knowledge by comparing what she knows to his vast and worldly experiences. He regularly reminds her of how superior he is to her because of these limited experiences. Rather than respond to his wife's experiences and feelings with openness and support, the husband attempts to inflate his position of power over her through rage, criticism, minimizing, and devaluing.

The following are some of the more common forms of domination as it is practiced in relationships with self and others. Emotional domination occurs when there is a physical and emotional withdrawal, which can be motivated by a need to punish one's self or another. Psychological domination can materialize when appointing someone other than one's self the responsibility for one's contentment and well being. Spiritual domination can arise when an expectation or demand is placed on another individual that he or she worship the same deity or practice the same religion as the individual who imposes the expectation or demand. Sexual domination can occur when an individual commands or demands that another individual engage in sexual activity against that individual's will. Physical domination arises when one individual threatens or inflicts bodily harm on another individual for reasons of degradation, abuse, and control.

Economic domination is controlling and restricting another person's ability to be economically responsible for one's self. Legal domination is the attempt to restrict an individual to a subordinate and inferior socioeconomic position. An example would be the elimination of Affirmative Action programs, a move that helps to perpetuate the practice of racial, gender, and economic segregation. Political domination occurs when effort is exerted to maintain ideological control over others. An example would be the traditional Democratic party's ward system whereby precinct captains hand out favors or food to maintain the loyalties of party members. Another example would be the insistence by both Democratic and Republican parties that in order to be a "good party member," one must vote a "straight party ticket."

When a relationship, either with self or another, is based on the practice of domination, conflict and disputes that arise are apt to be more intense and potentially abusive. This is a result of resentment, bitterness, and rage adversely influencing the conflict, thereby producing cruelty, and sometimes violence. The insertion of these emotions

Who We Are

into the conflict are directly akin to an internal belief held by the individual exhibiting cruelty, hatred, and violence that he or she is *something less than good*. For example, an attempt to introduce equality and mutuality into a relationship where the use of domination was once considered appropriate can incite resentment, bitterness, or rage between one partner, group, or community to another.

The reactionary behavior impedes the ability of the individuals involved to arrive at a palatable solution for the initial concern, which was establishing equality and mutuality in the relationship. More importantly, the reactionary behavior serves to keep the status quo in effect: power, control, and dominance. The immediate benefit for the persons who would limit or restrict the natural flow of feelings, thoughts, or actions of one's self and another is to maintain a position of power and dominance.

This translates into emotional, psychological, spiritual, sexual, physical, political, legal, or economic gain. The gain, which is to victimize, is indeed a perverse one that encourages an individual to usurp the integrity and dignity of one's self and another through coercive behavior. Domination has no need for cooperation and reconciliation because absolute power is the ultimate goal of the individual who seeks it.

What We Are

The practice of domination is a way of life that only an individual who believes that his or her essence and basic nature is either *something other than good*, *bad*, or *evil* would opt to use in relationships. The need to dominate another individual or one's self is motivated by a deep sense of personal weakness and inferiority. There is little or no sense of one's innate worth and value as a person, because there is the absence of knowing that he or she is the embodiment of good. Painfully speaking, the only way to experience personal worth and legitimacy, authority, and oftentimes prestige is to engage in the dominance and power game.

We have yet to learn that the model of domination creates experiences that can only end in humiliation, degrading manipulation, and abusive behavior. While on the contrary, the model of cooperation creates for an individual internal empowerment and autonomy. To live one's life from this place of personal good can pave the way for mutual and equal relationships to occur that exude emotional integrity and dignity.

Jean Shinoda Bolen, M.D. presents excellent insights concerning the issue of power in her book, *Ring of Power: The Abandoned Child, The Authoritarian Father, and The*

Disempowered Feminine. Bolen states: "Power over others serves psychologically as a means of obtaining a sense of security by having more power than others. Psychologically, power over others is also sought in order to feel superior, a goal that compensates for underlying feelings of inferiority. Power over others is also exercised to ward off feeling little, insignificant, or weak and is responsible for the sadistic belittling behavior on the part of people with power."

What has evolved as a popular approach to resolving personal and interpersonal conflict is to argue and debate symptoms, rather than exhibit the courage to address the root cause creating the conflict. This particular approach to problem solving propels us to merely adapt and adjust to the problem, thereby establishing a way of life that warrants a person being dominated by the problem. We take this approach to problem solving because it distracts us from addressing the root cause to our personal and interpersonal problems. And that root cause is the inner acceptance by an individual that his or her essence and basic nature is either *something other than good, bad,* or *evil*. Hence, we have the basis and motivation for the practice of domination.

What We Are

What further distracts us from achieving sensible solutions for our personal and interpersonal problems, especially of a societal nature, is our tendency of late to consult only with *experts*. These individuals are deemed valid for consultation because of specified training, credentials, and position. *What* an individual is determines his or her legitimacy as an *expert*. Tragically so, legitimacy is not determined by how effective a person has become in his or her life with setting forth an essence and basic nature that is undeniably good. I find it disturbing that legitimacy is not based on a commitment to live one's life enhancing and advancing the integrity, dignity, and autonomy of an individual's community, a community that includes this country and all its citizens.

Legitimacy is established by a willingness to face the intense struggle of bringing forth one's embodiment of good into a way of life in which seduction and illusion attempt to have an individual believe the opposite. Legitimacy means having the courage to act as the guardian not only of one's own right to experience his or her inherent good, but that of another individual as well. The standards that determine legitimacy would necessarily include a personal conviction to live one's life based on *who* he or she is innately. This individual would then profoundly understand

Who We Are

that *who* he or she is intrinsically is firmly implanted in that which is undeniably good.

Our society has demonstrated since the mid-1980s, an obsession with position, prestige, and academic credentials, somehow connecting this external validation with internal legitimacy. This gives an impression that we are conferring with our *best and brightest* to earnestly seek solutions for personal and interpersonal conflicts, particularly when there is a societal crisis. However, this obsession overshadows a very important point. A wealth of unbiased dialog and information is not likely to be found amongst those individuals deemed our *best and brightest* primarily because of an investment in *what* they are.

When conferring mainly with the *best and brightest,* a major stumbling block to arriving at viable solutions to societal issues, or issues judged to be of significance, is that their opinions are usually driven by political and economic agendas. What we, as lay people, are exposed to primarily comprises discussions and gatherings full of *who can shout louder than the other* and *who can condemn more effectively.*

Using the media as an example, on any given evening from Monday through Friday, a viewer can watch

What We Are

one of at least fifteen cable talk shows hosted by remarkably intelligent individuals. *Hardball with Chris Matthews, Rivera Live, The News with Brian Williams, Hockenberry, The Larry King Live Show, The O'Reilly Factor, Equal Time, Hannity & Colmes, Charles Grodin,* and *Charlie Rose* just to name a few. I must also add that the invited guests who appear on these shows are also exceptionally intelligent and can articulate their views and opinions quite well.

However, discussing and arriving at real causes or practical solutions for problems seem very remote when compared to the political and economic agenda-driven opinions that are being discussed among our *best and brightest*. Included in these discussions are vicious verbal attacks that are directed at any individual thought to oppose a particular view. A model of cooperation that recognizes the importance of dignity, integrity, and respect is not observed being initiated by either the hosts of these talk shows or their guests.

The only exceptions that I have experienced while viewing these shows are the *Larry King Live Show, Charles Grodin,* and *Charlie Rose.* These three talk shows expose the viewing audience to hosts who are gracious and respectable of others even though guests during interviews are often not. At one point during earlier telecast of *This Week*, with Cokie Roberts and Sam Donaldson, these two individuals exemplified gracious and ethical hosts. However, since the President Clinton scandal, they, along with George Will and Bill Kristol, have joined the ranks of condemning and demonizing journalists.

Outside of the *Larry King Show*, *Charles Grodin*, and *Charlie Rose*, the majority of talk shows have become nothing more than forums for witnessing the practice of domination. As the viewing audience is observing blatant exercises in domination, these talk shows posture for us a pretense that real solutions are being sought. For example, solutions dispassionately argued and debated on these programs in response to the issue of increased violence and cruelty in the public schools mainly focus on three immaterial points: the banning or restricting of guns, bringing prayer back into the schools, and getting more children back into the Christian churches.

When guns are used to threaten, to punish, and ultimately to end human life, this represents an unfortunate digression of behavior rather than a progression in our society with respect to resolving conflict. In an earlier time, because there was widespread lawlessness, the answer

What We Are

was more guns. Today, I would like to think of our society as having evolved to a more civilized state with respect to resolving differences and conflict. Yet the continued reaction to lawlessness or stated another way, the escalation of dominance, is still more guns. Violence and cruelty are used to perpetuate a way of life that is based on the practice of domination, and guns are being used to serve the same purpose. Therefore, it is the manner in which guns are being used in American society that should be our collective focus, not whether gun usage should be restricted or that guns be eliminated.

Furthermore, the use of guns will never be restricted in this country nor will it be eliminated; guns are and have been a significant part of the American culture and its history. Guns are synonymous with the tough and invincible image America has consistently sought to portray since its inception. The manner in which guns are used in our society by an increasing number of individuals constitutes a mechanism to perpetuate the use of domination and the control of one individual over another. And the individual who would seek to dominate another person or self in this manner is acting out a lie that he or she has accepted internally. The lie is that this individual believes that he or she is the embodiment of an essence and basic

Who We Are

nature that is *evil*; this is the core issue that deserves our fullest attention and is propelling the destructive use of guns in our society.

Bringing prayer back into the schools or getting more children into Christian Churches misses the point dramatically, as well. Teaching our children about Christian ideology while at the same time teaching them the appropriateness of domination in their relationships is exposing them to more adult absurdity. Once more, we do not approach personal and interpersonal problems from a standpoint of ascertaining its cause. Our inclination is to become ensnared in a complex environment of implication and intimation. I firmly believe this is why "the more things change, the more they remain the same."

As I mentioned earlier, a person will practice domination of others and self as a result of accepting a self-perception that he or she is either *something other than good*, *bad*, or *evil*. What this also exemplifies is that the individual who engages in this particular behavior does so because he or she is emotionally weak and socially dependent. Even though there will be a concerted effort to project a public demeanor or posture that will convey the opposite self-perception, the internalized weakness and dependency will be recognizable.

What We Are

What will steadily reveal itself is the reluctance and sometimes absolute refusal to have compassion for an individual who is inclined to commit errors in judgement and who exhibits weak and dependent behavior. Experiencing another individual's imperfections is a constant reminder of this individual's *less than good* perception of self. This person could be a man, woman, or child, and he or she is prone to dominate anyone who exhibits these behaviors. During moments of internal or external conflict, no one is safe from the harsh and critical behavior that can be exhibited by these individuals.

This emotional distress is <u>further intensified by an internal acceptance that he or she is unworthy and undeserving of the personal effort to develop a perception of self that is based on the truth of *who* he or she is innately</u>. The effort in question is the personal work that is necessary to undertake in order to gain awareness and acceptance of one's self. Specifically, this entails developing the knowledge and acceptance that one's essential qualities and basic nature that define *who* one is as a person is undeniably good. To live from this place of one's inherent authority, legitimacy, and autonomy requires the steadfast acceptance that one's personal essence is undeniably good.

Who We Are

This allows an individual to know and demonstrate *who* she or he is, and this will always take precedence and value over *what* an individual is externally. A person will always recognize immediately when he or she is actualizing this particular conviction. Again, there will be a personal commitment to be the guardian of one's own and another's dignity, autonomy, and respect. There are direct links between experiencing one's essence as good, living one's life with dignity and emotional integrity, and living *who* one is intrinsically. This way of life is made viable because the individual has accepted without question that his or her essence and basic nature is good.

It simply is not an established practice in American society to raise our children to know and to accept that their essence and basic nature is unmistakably good. Neither is it an established practice to raise our children to accept a personal commitment to live from this same authentic place. Regretfully so, these are not established practices because neither is an established practice for adults. For a child to know and accept that his or her personal essence is good, the adults who comprise a child's environment must verbally inform him or her of the unique and essential qualities that comprise this good. Recognition

What We Are

of this nature is what encourages and supports a child to live his or her life based on *who* the child is innately.

In American society, we do not make a distinction between *who* an individual is and his or her behavior; we link the two together. Since recognition of an individual is primarily performance oriented, a child learns that he or she is good if performance or behavior satisfies expectations, and bad if they do not. Rather than recognize and accept *who* a person is, which would promote the emotional and spiritual development of a person's essence, we instead place a great deal of importance on compliance and performance.

This is the difference between a *good person* and a *nice person*. The *nice person* is emotionally and spiritually separated from knowing that his or her essence and basic nature is good. This is the premise for the *nice* behavior. Due to a lack of knowing that one's essence and basic nature is good, this person will invest a considerable amount of emotional and religious energy in an attempt to maintain a belief that his or her essence and basic nature is good. Usually this energy is exhibited through fanaticism and rituals. However, the power of a person's ego can never convert what has already become an internal belief on emotional and spiritual levels. And that internal belief is that one's essence and basic nature is either *something other than good, bad, or evil*.

For the individual who has learned to be *nice,* recognition and acceptance on the basis of *who* she or he is during the formative and developmental stages was not provided. Instead, the recognition and acceptance that was experienced by this individual existed primarily on the basis of performance and conformity. As a result of this particular child-rearing practice, the innate qualities of this individual remain undeveloped, which means *who* this person is cannot be experienced in his or her environment.

Stated another way, the individuality of this person remains undeveloped because there is a lack of adult mirrors and echoes to reflect back to this person *who* he or she is innately. And since recognition and acceptance was learned as being based on performance and conformity, the child and adolescent then tailors and shapes his or her life based on a *what* principle. In other words, *what* this individual is carries a greater significance and personal value than *who* this individual is innately. It will not be until well into one's adulthood that the realization of this betrayal to one's self will be felt as a heart-breaking awareness.

What We Are

With all the effort that an individual invests in the social cover of *nice* behavior, it is practically, if not altogether, nonexistent when one particular experience occurs. A *nice person* ceases to be nice when he or she experiences either internal or external conflict. Because being nice is a learned behavior, it becomes difficult to maintain this behavior once a stronger impulse takes center stage, emotionally speaking. That stronger impulse is to react, rather than respond when experiencing either internal or external conflict.

We are also taught as a child and adolescent through adult modeling to view internal and external conflict from an adversarial position. The tendency is to become antagonistic, combative, and hurtful to others or one's self through the usage of one or more of the eight forms of domination. It then becomes a necessity to practice domination and control in order to overcompensate for feeling either *something other than good, bad, or evil*. As a result of exerting this distorted sense of authority and power, an individual is able to experience self-importance through self-indulgent behavior. This is unfortunate, because at that moment of truth there is no awareness and least of all no acceptance of one's essence and basic nature as being undeniably good.

Who We Are

It should be pointed out that not everyone who experiences rejection with respect to *who* he or she is during the formative and developmental stages will choose to incorporate *nice* behavior into his or her way of life. Widespread numbers of individuals in our society choose to incorporate *nice* behavior into their way of life because it is expected of them. A sure way for an individual to gain social acceptance and have one's environment respond with approval is to act kind, compassionate, loving, and avoid conflicts.

However, not everyone is interested nor invested in social acceptance. The individual who chooses a demeanor that is contrary to *nice* does so for specific reasons. This person accepts that his or her essence and basic nature is either *bad* or *evil,* because personal experiences have primarily consisted of degradation, debasement, and humiliation. If one's personal experiences result in personal humiliation for long periods of time, then that individual will eventually perceive himself or herself as *bad* or *evil.*

Thus, there simply is no need to conform to popular belief with respect to acceptable behavior. This individual has deemed himself or herself as unacceptable, more than likely because he or she was treated as unacceptable.

51

What We Are

Neither is there a need to feel accepted by his or her family of origin, community, or society. As a matter of fact, this individual will seek to establish or join a peer group that will reflect similar beliefs as to an essence and basic nature that is *bad* or *evil*.

An individual who has learned to be a *nice* person, generally speaking, will have a self-perception that he or she is *something other than good* or *bad*. One major characteristic of a *nice person* is the inability to forgive either self or others for mistakes involving moral issues. Since there is an ongoing internal antagonism with accepting that one's essence and basic nature is good, there is very little, if any, forgiveness of self and others. There is a harshness that accompanies the inability to forgive, especially when it comes to issues of morality.

For example, the condemnation and demonization surrounding both Hillary Clinton and her husband, President Clinton, during their time in the White House was staggering. Attack after attack, which was unmerciful, has been undertaken against these two as individuals rather than against their behavior. There is no question that both individuals have displayed public behavior while in office that is considered unethical and unacceptable. However, neither Hillary nor President Clinton deserved to be treated with the lack of dignity, integrity, and respect this country witnessed during their time in the Oval Office.

Another distinguishing characteristic of a *nice person* is the insistence that others prove that they are trustworthy before he or she can feel safe. The stratagem is to seduce and induce those individuals comprising one's primary relationships into taking responsibility for creating a safe relationship before this person can trust the other persons in the relationship. The *nice person* wants to make the issue of trust the responsibility of someone other than one's self because there is an ongoing internal conflict over accepting that one's essence and basic nature is good. Other people will need to prove that they are trustworthy because this individual is influenced by the internal lie that he or she is unworthy of intimacy.

On the other hand, the individual who knows that he or she is a good person is emotionally and spiritually accepting that his or her essence and basic nature is undeniably good. And for this very reason this individual can maintain that personal truth throughout the presence of internal and external conflict. This individual refuses to view one's self or another as an adversary or enemy. He or she is committed to emotional integrity, and protects the dignity of self and others. Experiences with self and others that involve forgiveness and trust are not an enigma. This person understands that the very essence and basic nature of each and every individual is fundamentally good.

There is an awareness and acceptance by the individual who knows that he or she is the embodiment of good that painful experiences occurring during the formidable and developmental stages can adversely affect a person. He or she understands that experiences that deny or impede the emergence of *who* an individual is can encourage that person to internally accept an essence that is *less than good*.

There is also an acceptance that personal responsibility for behavior that is detrimental to the well being of self and others is absolutely necessary. Furthermore, the *good person* knows without a doubt that an individual need not be emotionally murdered or condemned for behavior that is inappropriate or detrimental to the well being of self and others. A *good person* knows that it is proper to deem such behavior as an error in judgement, and not deem either self or another person as a mistake.

Who We Are

With so much emphasis being placed on performance, dominance, and control in our society today, an individual is not apt to be willing to change this particular lifestyle until she or he has reached the mid- to late forties. By the time a person reaches this period in his or her life, there is a possibility of acknowledging a personal lack of fulfillment due to exhaustion and overwhelming disappointment as the result of practicing domination and control. Counseling or therapy could get an individual there much sooner, which would be motivated by having accumulated enough broken and pain-filled relationships due to the practice of domination.

Since there is less effort directed toward developing *who* we are as individuals, it makes perfect sense why we expend great effort and energy developing a way of life based on *what* we are. We have succumbed to a way of thinking that suggests that an individual reaches his or her greatest potential as the result of fulfilling a *what* principle. *What* an individual is pertains directly to a role that he or she agrees to comply with, including its established standards for behavior. Examples of such roles include husband, wife, stockbroker, postal clerk, fashion designer, son, daughter, airplane pilot, lover, and neighbor.

What We Are

Excelling in a way of life that is primarily based on *what* we are simply means that an individual has been successful in practicing one or more forms of domination. For example, the major league baseball pitcher who is compensated with a $105 million salary for pitching every fifth day, versus the high school teacher who is compensated with a salary of $39,000 for teaching five days a week. Our incessant need to be entertained has lead our society to be emotionally and psychologically dominated, in particular, by the institution of sports.

The conviction to live one's life based on *who* that individual is can provide economic, emotional, and spiritual success. Just as important, this success will not be at the cost of one's own or another person's dignity, integrity, or respect. The success is authentic because the essence, the highest quality of good that a person embodies, is present promoting mutuality and respect. Success occurs across the board because everyone involved is morally and spiritually enhanced.

On any given day of the week countless numbers of people wake up in the morning and begin a ritual that prepares them for the journey to their place of employment. These same individuals spend a good portion of their day

Who We Are

at a place of employment where support and reward is provided to them in relation to how successful he or she can perform under a *what* principle. At the end of the workday, these same individuals return to their homes prepared to experience a very different way of life. At home, success in their primary relationships is determined by how well they function within the *who* principle.

This is still true for the individual who is returning home and is not in a primary relationship. <u>Success in one's relationship with self is determined by how well that person can function within the *who* principle.</u> Granted, there are numerous relationships in our society that are not based or concerned with a *who* principle because the relationships are based on a model of domination. Hence, issues of mutuality, respect, and emotional integrity are of no concern, which is perfectly within their right to experience.

However, for those individuals who are concerned about the issues of mutuality, dignity, and emotional integrity, there begins a major conflict as they prepare for the workday. The conflict for many of these individuals occurs when leaving home cloaked in a role that will satisfy their employer, but that is in opposition to the basic nature or essence of the individual. The morning ritual includes the

What We Are

task of setting aside sentiments of integrity and accountability that are the vanguard to such interests as mutuality, dignity, and authenticity. Bolen adds: "Whenever obedience to power is emphasized, feelings and thoughts that lead to independent behavior and compassion for others are systematically suppressed. Being loved and loving others have no place in power-based institutions (and a family can be one)."

This adult conflict is quite similar to the conflict that children are exposed to when informed of the appropriateness of domination over an opponent and the need for cooperation to ensure team success. The dilemma that is played out during the morning hours as an adult has its roots in childhood, where it was learned that *who* you are cannot accompany what you do. There is a direct link between the practice of domination and what we are; neither can exist without the other. The compromise that an individual agrees to in response to not being encouraged or allowed to live from a place of *who,* is to learn how to be a *nice person*. Again, not every individual is willing to learn this behavior after being informed either covertly or overtly that *who* she or he is cannot be allowed into the environment.

Who We Are

For those able to make the painful shift during the morning routine in preparation for work, being nice under any and all circumstances must replace being good. It is important to remember that recognition and reward is primarily based on how well one performs in a role. That role is economic in nature, and being good may interfere with that economic agenda. There is a direct relationship between salary, wages, and revenue that is profit orientated, and this relationship should never be construed otherwise.

It has been suggested, and rather strongly I might add, that a viable solution for those individuals faced with such a dilemma seek self-employment, then this problem of opposing philosophies would no longer exist. My response to this particular stance is that this remedy certainly is working quite well for a number of working-class people. However, self-employment does not guarantee that the practice of domination would be nonexistent, nor does it guarantee that an individual would opt to work from a place of *who* she or he is intrinsically.

And since the numbers would be so high, our society could nor would not support philosophically and economically a huge influx of working-class people moving into the ranks of the self-employed. Current bureaucratic agencies

What We Are

and tax laws barely support the self-employed and small business entrepreneur now, so this condition would only become more frustrating and produce more anger for both the bureaucratic agencies and the self-employed.

Being nice and competent in one's role at work helps to ensure that the working environment is comfortable so that one can fully concentrate on matters at hand: protecting and increasing revenues. Respect and camaraderie is more likely to occur as a result of generating revenue or providing excellent support to those that do generate revenue. One fact is for certain: there is a close relationship between economic domination and being a successful business enterprise in our society.

For example, wages earned are very seldom equal to labor output. And this can work in favor of the employer as well as the employee. Take the sub-par year that the $105 million pitcher, Kevin Brown had for the Dodgers during the 1999 baseball season. Working roughly every fifth day, he was unable to help the Dodgers achieve their goal of reaching the play-offs and the World Series, because he was in part not as effective as he had been prior to signing his lucrative contract. However, the Dodger organization, despite paying Mr. Brown a ridiculous salary to pitch basically once a week, was still financially successful. The Dodger brass could make this claim due to the baseball fan's willingness to support this form of economic domination by either paying the high-ticket prices or watching the sub-par performance on cable or local television.

Throughout the workplace the practice of domination in one form or another can be observed with consistency. Generally speaking, the lower one is on the scale of importance, the greater the incident of domination. It is unfortunate that, even though domination and control will advance from those with authority and power down to those with little or none, it flourishes among those who have the least amount of power. In other words, those individuals having the least authority and power in the workplace tend to oppress one another with unconscionable cruelty and domination.

For instance, a personal secretary who has been on the job for less than a year. She opens her boss's mail as part of her daily responsibilities, only to discover a racist and sexist joke that is sent to him by a friend. When the secretary informs her boss how she felt impacted by the offensiveness of the joke, the boss emotionally and mentally abuses the secretary and threatens her with immediate

What We Are

termination for reading his mail. He makes certain that the office personnel, which are the secretary's peers, are made aware of the conflict by informing a woman who has been with the company the longest.

Since this woman is extremely loyal to her boss, she organizes the rest of the office personal to support their employer. Within two hours, the secretary is treated with indignity and ignored for a week by the entire group. The anger and rage a person experiences as a result of being dominated is directed towards others who are also being dominated rather than towards the source of domination. Behavior such as this renders an individual's justifiable anger and rage as impotent.

It is fascinating to observe how individuals with the greatest amount of authority and power in the workplace have a tendency to work hard at portraying themselves as extremely nice and even as good people. Yet, we all are aware that in order for a person to reside in a position of moderate to notable authority and power, someone or some people necessarily had to be dominated for this to occur. It is my contention that an individual who accepts his or her essence or basic nature as good will not accept position or money that has come as a result of sexual, racial, or economic domination. A person who accepts his or her essence or basic nature as good will not forget that he or she is also the guardian of another person's integrity, dignity, and respect.

Because the practice of domination is a way of life at the workplace, the further down on the scale of importance an individual is, the more that being good becomes a liability. An individual is apt to be the recipient of contempt and hatred from coworkers and superiors. Being good could be construed as weakness, since domination is primarily concerned about preying on the weak and vulnerable. Being nice helps to keep away some contempt and hatred out of a person's face, since it can be easily forsaken when conflict occurs.

On the contrary, the higher up an individual is in terms of importance, the less he or she will need to concern themselves with the practice of domination as it pertains to the infrastructure. Remember that these individuals can always find someone on which to project the fallout that the practice of domination creates. This does not mean that the practice of domination is absent as one moves up the scale of importance, it only means that it is less petty and more lethal. Competition for positions offering more power by individuals already in power can be one of the most debasing and debilitating experiences a person can encounter. There is no emotional integrity and accountability; respect for personage is a lost virtue.

I fully realize that I have spent the last several paragraphs making broad and sweeping generalizations regarding the practice of domination in the workplace. I fully realize as well that not every employer and employee in the workplace is going to engage in the type of domination that I have described. My intent is to point out what I have come to learn does exist for many employers and employees in the workplace. I apologize to those employers and employees who are committed to a practice of integrity, respect, and dignity in the workplace if I have overstated my personal and professional observations.

There is an expectation that has gained considerable momentum during the past decade, and it has also become a major source of personal frustration and disappointment for the individual who subscribes to its implication. A number of people are under the notion that because they are successful and prosperous in their academic pursuits, social circles, and careers, this success should of course carry over into their primary relationships.

Who We Are

It is a mistake to make this assumption, unless the individuals involved in the primary relationship have agreed to base their relationship on domination; then, all is well.

For individuals who have not achieved an impressive resume of outstanding success and prosperity with respect to academic pursuits, social circles, and career endeavors, no such correlation is formed. However, the same problem confronts this individual, and that is, how to effectively negotiate the balancing act between the *what* and *who* ways of life.

Relationships outside of the workplace, especially at home, are where many individuals want to experience support and love for *who* they are with respect to their essence and basic nature. But this can be a frustrating experience with disappointing results. It is difficult to juggle both worlds, especially when the *what* you are way of life is so quick to reward with money and power for being beautiful, handsome, obedient, and dominated as opposed to the *who* way of life.

It is important to know that the development of an individual's personal authority cannot take place unless the practice of accountability is taking place simultaneously.

What We Are

Accountability is an absolute must in order for the model of cooperation to be effective. Accountability preserves the credibility of the individual who provides it, as well the integrity of the individual receiving it. It is accountability that gives passion and meaning to the phrase that we are indeed the guardians of our own and another's dignity and respect. Accountability is simply having the emotional integrity to share or expound upon one's behavior, experiences, and feelings to either self or with another individual.

Granted, there are instances when it is not in the best interest of the individuals involved for accountability to take place with respect to behavior, experiences, and feelings. What may appear on the surface to be a move towards a healing process can actually be an experience that creates more unnecessary suffering. This can occur for both the individual who is being accountable, and to the individual who is the recipient of another's accountability. Not everyone who has been hurt or harmed by the actions of another individual is open to hearing accountability, no matter how sincere or genuine the apology. The refusal to hear or accept accountability by an injured person from the individual responsible for a painful experience has to be respected, but this will not limit or restrict achieving the aim of accountability.

Who We Are

Humility is always the desired intent of accountability. It is the body and soul's healing agent. Humility is the heartfelt compassion, forgiveness, and serenity that a person experiences when emotionally open to the acceptance of one's own humanity. Self-redemption is made possible only because the individual is emotionally open to the experience of humility. Emotional integrity is the principle that motivates a person to be accountable for his or her behavior, experiences, and feelings, thereby making it possible to experience humility. This is when an individual comes to learn that his or her imperfection is actually one's perfection, and that grace is the outward manifestation of the embodiment of humility.

I continue to believe that the strongest challenge that American society will face in the twenty-first century will be if we, as a society, can effectively live with one another as a cohesive community. Personal and interpersonal relationships are going to be strongly challenged as a result of our society's way of life continuing to impose a high premium on wealth, greed, and domination. The need to achieve these goals, which are external of self, will continue to outdistance the need to achieve emotional integrity and personal dignity.

What We Are

The youth of American society will continue to be exposed at younger and younger ages to the high premiums that are placed on the accumulation of wealth, power, and greed. As a direct result of this over-stimulation, we will continue to experience from our children an increase in violence, cruelty, and the need to dominate other individuals. A lack of emotional, intellectual, and spiritual skills will be a major contributing factor as well, because sophistication will not be a forte of our young people.

A component that is absolutely necessary for creating cohesiveness in personal and interpersonal relationships is emotional integrity. Emotional integrity can motivate a person to know more about *who* one's self and another is with respect to his or her essence or basic nature. This experience encourages an individual to understand the *story* that a person embodies. Yet, within personal and interpersonal relationships this component seems notably absent, especially when internal or external conflict is present. For the most part, relationships in our society seem fused together by fear, power, and intimidation rather than by integrity, dignity, and respect.

Simply being willing to *show up*, to be emotionally present in one's life or another is one of the more difficult extensions of self we seem to struggle with, both individually and collectively, in American society. To personify emotional integrity necessarily translates into a willingness to accept total responsibility for one's life. Accepting total responsibility for one's life means accepting responsibility for his or her behavior, decisions, passions, and consequences.

Emotional integrity includes accountability for behavior and how that behavior may impact another person or a group of people. Integrity also includes a commitment to preserve the nobility of character with respect to one's self and that of another individual. To practice emotional integrity and personal responsibility in one's life translates into dignity and respect for self and others. This is autonomy and personal legitimacy made manifest in a person's life.

Accountability is the moral fiber that holds a family, community, and country together as a cohesive unit. Without its presence and influence, there is a breakdown among its members with respect to civilized behavior toward one another. Humility, personal authority, and autonomy are replaced with arrogance, power, and entanglement. As we continue to mirror before our children a model of domination, we also teach them through example how to avoid accountability and personal responsibility for one's life, which includes the issue of change. Children continue to learn from adults a luxury that is corrupt, which calls for the using of someone or something as a primary focus for determining the source of one's conflict or problem.

In summary, it is not difficult to understand why we continue to experience enormous complications in resolving issues of conflict in our society. It makes no difference whether the issues are personal, interpersonal, or societal in nature. The overall experience continues to be the same condemnation, demonization, and agenda-driven solutions that we have become so accustomed to hearing over the past several decades. The end result that continues to survive time and time again is the commitment to the practice of domination in our relationships, in all its various forms.

The obstacles that prevent us from truly resolving personal, interpersonal, and societal issues can easily be detected in our current approach to internal and external conflict. Conflict is viewed as an adversarial experience and one to avoid. Unfortunately, both views are far from the truth of conflict. Conflict is a teacher and its purpose is to help us to experience more and more of our true essence and basic nature, which is invariably established in good. Conflict helps to teach an individual more about herself or himself by presenting situations that will expose what is undeveloped within the personality and in need of development.

An example would be a man's or woman's request that a friendship shift to a romantic relationship. As a result of the offer being declined, there is a reaction of depression, anger, and resentment directed at the person declining the offer on the part of the person who requested the shift. What was once a caring and giving friendship has become adversarial, and the friendship is now in jeopardy. The person requesting the shift in the relationship internalizes that he or she is *not good enough* and is an *unworthy* person. The person who has declined the offer internalizes that he or she is responsible for hurting someone profoundly cared about.

Both individuals personalize this experience and spiral downward internally because the essence or basic nature of *who* he or she is, which is solid and good, is not recognized nor accepted as such. To feel hurt and disappointment that the offer was declined is appropriate. To feel sad about saying no to a friend's offer to shift a friendship to a romantic relationship is also appropriate. However,

What We Are

when this experience is personalized to such degrees, then the purpose of this conflict is defined.

The purpose is to teach both individuals more about their respective intrinsic value, which is adequate and worthy. It is to teach both individuals about personal autonomy, accountability, and the importance of viewing one's self as the true source of one's passion. Finally, this conflict teaches both individuals what is undeveloped within their personalities and needs to be developed. We know this to be especially true because there is a reaction and an overreaction to saying no and to experiencing no as a rejection on moral grounds, respectively. In general, if there is a response rather than a reaction or overreaction to conflict, then an individual can look at what his or her portion of the conflict may be, if any. The purpose of conflict is still served, which is to provide an opportunity to develop more of one's essence or basic nature. In this manner we move away from being merely concerned with the symptoms of a problem to discovering its root cause.

Another obstacle that prevents us from arriving at a viable solution to an issue is the refusal to accept responsibility and accountability for any part of the conflict. The model of domination, in order for it to be effective,

Who We Are

must be concerned with symptoms and not with causes, because then someone would have to accept responsibility. It is a model that produces victims. We teach our children to look outside of themselves for someone to blame or to find fault with, but then we expect them act differently than what is being mirrored before them. Rather than being taught to look at one's self to determine what part of her or his behavior, if any, could be contributing to the problem, our children lash out with destructive behavior, similar to that of adults. This approach to problem solving affords the opportunity to avoid getting at the root cause of the problem, and at the root of most personal and societal problems is the practice of some form of domination.

Nothing short of an absolute commitment to learn and accept the truth about ourselves, individually speaking, will reverse the escalating violence, cruelty, and indifference to human life that is currently engulfing our society. And that truth which each and every individual who comprises this American society embodies is that the very essence or basic nature is without question good. Our individual and collective histories, whether familial, ethnic, cultural, or religious has perpetuated a lie. The lie is how we were lead to believe that our individual essence or basic nature is either *something other than good, bad, or evil*. And this

What We Are

lie was a result of how each and every one of us as children, adolescents, and young adults were mistreated. We were mistreated because *who* we are, intrinsically speaking, was not recognized as basically good, nor were we encouraged to recognize this basic good about ourselves.

I am well aware that there are individuals within our society who do not fall into the above experiences because as children and adolescents they were treated with dignity and respect. To these individuals I say, how blessed you truly have been, but your help is sorely needed to insert a model of cooperation that replaces a model of domination in which others have greatly suffered. I know this to be true—that we all have personal and societal histories that are replete with information that our essence or basic nature was *something other than good*. Again, this was a lie. It is time to live the truth if we are to persist as a nation of diverse cultures and ethnicity during the twenty-first century.

The United States of America is truly a great country. Its greatness does not lie in its natural resources with respect to material goods. Its greatness lies in the fact that we espouse certain truths that support the freeing of an

Who We Are

individual's spirit and essence. We, as a society, promote on paper what the human spirit coupled with the human intellect proposes as every woman's, man's, and child's ultimate freedom: the freedom for an individual to be *who* she or he is intrinsically. We cannot afford to play down to our history as a society or to the rest of the world; friend or foe.

Today, the world looks to us to lead, to be the vanguard with respect to how to live with multiplicity, diversity, and meaning. We are trend-setters and role models for the rest of the world, whether we like it or not. We are a nation of many different peoples with different ethnicities, cultures, politics, economics, and religions. We need not dominate one another or other parts of the world because of our fear of these differences. It is our responsibility to demonstrate to ourselves and to the rest of the world that we know how to live with emotional integrity and dignity as a community and as a nation. Our time is now. Our destiny as a leader in world affairs now focuses itself on changing our internal and external models of domination to a model of cooperation that guarantees real freedom for good people.

What We Are

"Evil is created when myth is posed as reality to avoid the responsibility for decrying the lie."

Bradley Lee Ulrich

PART 2

UNDERSTANDING THE SOLUTION

What We Are

If you bring forth what is within you,
What you bring forth will save you.

If you do not bring forth what is within you,
What you do not bring forth will destroy you.

> Jesus
> (From the Book of Thomas)
> Gnostic Gospels

If the model by which we establish relationships is not replaced with a more appropriate model, issues gravely impacting our morality, both individually and as a society, are sure to escalate. Again, all that we need to do is witness our tendency to condemn, demonize, and commit violence when there is either internal or external conflict. The model of domination persists with interpreting virtues such as emotional integrity, personal dignity, autonomy, and accountability as irrelevant. On the other hand, a model of cooperation would guarantee the survival of these virtues that are necessary for the actual survival of humankind. If one is lost, the other cannot survive alone.

Who We Are

These virtues, if lost, will radically restrict our ability to experience an essence, individually and collectively, that is without question fundamentally solid and good. If we, as a society, are to remain committed to the basic rights and freedoms espoused in our founding documents, then these virtues need to be solidly incorporated into our way of life. Our founding documents justify our existence and purpose, and it is our responsibility to honor these documents with a vigilant commitment not to allow one person to experience indignity. The moral crisis that we are now in the grips of is the result of a way of life that has been systemically corrupted from its beginning by the practice of domination. The virtues that would ensure the cohesiveness of family, community, and nation can no longer be simply cast along the roadside of our society's continued evolution.

With that said, I will begin a brief journey into recent experiences as a writer and experiences as a young adolescent. Shortly after I began to write the manuscript for my first book in April of 1995, *RELATIONSHIPS: Shattering The Lies We Live By!,* I began to experience unusual and unnerving feelings. I was not certain what was happening to me, which made it difficult and at times impossible to articulate my internal conflict with any degree of coherency.

What We Are

At first, I thought that the feelings of shame, embarrassment, doubt, and fear were an internal response to writing about the issue of conflict. In particular, about how we, individually and as a society, view conflict as an adversarial experience and as one to avoid as much as possible. On one occasion I said to myself, "Of course I would feel shame, fear, embarrassment, and doubt. In addition to writing about conflict, I am also writing about the Judeo/Christian influence with respect to how we experience internal and external conflict. In effect, I am questioning one of our society's most sacred and powerful institutions: Christianity."

These intense feelings occurred again when I was in the process of writing the manuscript for *Abstract Freedom,* one year later. Again, I was able to rationalize the origin of these feelings. This time I was writing about our inability, individually and as a society, to experience integrity, dignity, and a genuine freedom as long as we refuse to be honest and truthful about the practice of domination as it pertains to women and Native and African Americans. The question I asked—and attempted to answer—in that book was: How can relationships be expected to provide a basis for integrity, dignity, and accountability when a history of abuse and injustice basically goes unrecognized as such, especially in our history books?

Who We Are

The basis on which the American way of life has been founded upon is the practice of dominating and controlling other individuals. Once again, we witness this practice, especially when the issue of conflict has occurred. This is what governs primary and secondary relationships, and domination is what perpetuates violent and cruel behavior. Again, I said to myself, "Of course I would feel shame, fear, embarrassment, and doubt. I am writing about the difficulty in experiencing integrity, dignity, and accountability in a society that has established a way of life based on the practice of domination. In addition, I am also writing about the European American male's influence with respect to the rules by which we establish our relationships, the rules of control and domination. And finally, I am questioning this society's most sacred and powerful individual and his way of life: the European American male."

It was not until I was in the middle of collaborating on the manuscript, *MADE FROM SCRATCH: A Recipe For Success* in May of 1999 that I began to make some sense of my internal conflict. At first, just like before, I began to experience the intense feeling of embarrassment. However, this time I did not experience the shame, fear, and doubt that accompanied the two previous writing exercises. I mumbled to myself, "What made this experience different,

What We Are

except for the obvious?" The obvious was that I was collaborating on the autobiography of an Italian American woman.

Her inspiring story revealed how she overcame various personal and cultural obstacles after immigrating to this country from the southern portion of Italy as a little girl. As a young woman, she married a fine young Italian American man, and together they became successful restaurant entrepreneurs. The import of her story lies in the essence and spirit of this woman. Success as a restaurant entrepreneur was the result of a conviction to live her life in full knowledge and acceptance that her essence is fundamentally solid and good.

Nella, as family, friends, and customers know her, knew without a doubt that she is a *good person* and that she was firmly committed to living her life from this standpoint. This included the acceptance that the dignity, integrity, and autonomy of other people, whether they were family, friend, or stranger, warranted her recognition as well. Putting into action a model of cooperation is the secret to Nella's success both as a woman and businesswoman. Her way of life continues to stand up to the test of time.

Who We Are

Nella knew conflict and she knew it all too well. She came upon it daily, living and working in male-dominated communities that wanted to restrict her right to experience her solvency as a woman and businesswoman. What empowered Nella to see her way through conflicts growing up as a child, adolescent, and young adult was the ability to remain anchored in her basic nature and essence. Rather than spiral downward emotionally and spiritually, she remained firm in the truth that she is fundamentally a *good person*. Her refusal to condemn, blame, or find fault with either herself or other people have been consistent virtues of Nella.

It was the telling of Ornella Curatolo's story that provided me with insight into my internal conflict. And when I personally met Nella, one early afternoon in Chicago, I immediately pieced together the difference between a *nice person* and a *good person*. I discovered that Nella and Jack, her husband, were *good people*. I was able to observe firsthand while at their place of business, Nella and Jack experiencing numerous conflicts both of a personal and business nature.

What I came away with that was refreshing and uplifting was how both Nella and Jack could remain anchored in an essence of good, and yet experience the fullness of each conflict. They both could experience their respective anger, disappointment, and hurt without feeling a need to condemn, find fault, or blame. As a result of collaborating to write Nella's autobiography and personally meeting Jack and her, I was now able to understand exactly what had been occurring within me for the past four years.

My intense feelings of fear, doubt, and embarrassment had nothing to do with what I was writing in the three books. For the first time in my life I began to experience my own essence or basic nature. What was causing my internal disturbance was that I was experiencing an essence that was fundamentally solid and good. The unnerving feelings that were engulfing my body and mind for four years were emotional reactions to these new perceptions of myself—new perceptions that were being developed as I was reconnecting with my true and real essence. A perception that I am legitimate, competent, equal, and that I embody a personal authority based on *who* I am was now entering my conscious thinking.

For years on end I have portrayed myself in such a way as to give the impression that I believed that I embodied these perceptions. However, what I actually believed was that my essence or basic nature was *something other than good*, that is, weak, passive, inadequate, and less than. I could look and act the part that I was a *nice person*. And if someone asked me if I thought that my essence was good, I would respond in the affirmative with a righteous indignation. Still and all, it was always so easy for me to betray my façade. I would easily lose the façade of a *nice person* who portrayed that his essence was good when either internal or external conflict entered my world.

Blame, condemnation, cruel statements that were meant to hurt, and finding fault with either myself or someone else abruptly replaced the *nice person* façade. Today I have come to understand that there is a vast difference between believing and knowing; it is as different as day and night. The difference is what separates the *nice person* from the individual who knows that he or she is a *good person*. One is grounded in power and control. The other is a truth that is grounded in an essence that is basically good.

The new perceptions were a dramatic contradiction to what I had internalized about myself as a result of childhood, adolescence, and young adulthood experiences. For over forty years of my life I have carried inside of me perceptions that I was illegitimate, inferior, weak, passive,

What We Are

and lacking self-confidence. During my writing experiences, what had been occurring within me was a literal transformation. It was a transformation that occurs when a person moves from believing a truth about himself or herself to knowing that truth on an emotional and spiritual level. My conscious thinking was being impacted by this new awareness of myself.

I was totally unaware that I was transitioning out of an emotional and spiritual place, one in which I viewed my essence to be *something other than good*. I was not conscious that I was transitioning into an emotional and spiritual place that was never acknowledged or accepted by me relative to *who* I am. The fact that I am generous, kind, compassionate, passionate, loving, intelligent, community-minded, and unconditional in my love for myself and others had failed to be accepted by me as part of my essence. Even though there had been people in my life who had informed me of these qualities and more, I simply could not hear this information. Until such time that I could actually experience these qualities myself, nothing ever registered on an emotional and spiritual level that my essence was fundamentally good.

Earlier in my life, late teens to the age of thirty, I actually did perceive my essence to be *evil* and *bad*. These perceptions were the direct result of my alcoholism and drug addiction years. Fortunately for me, recovery helped to dispel these particular lies. However, I never did move beyond the perception that my essence was *something other than good.* This was the next level after transitioning out of the *evil* and *bad* self-perceptions.

Much of my emotional and spiritual work evolved around my relationships with my parents. I was a stranger to my father, and my father was a stranger to me. I knew that he was an outstanding artist and a dedicated mail carrier for twenty-six years. He had a mother, brothers, sisters, and friends who cared deeply for him. I have heard many of these individuals say that my father was a great man, a good man, and a man who loved his family. This was always a big mystery for me. These individuals experienced my father in ways that I, his son, was not given the opportunity to experience. I often ponder what was great and good about my father, and why was it that I failed to experience his love? I knew *what* this man was, but I never, never knew *who* my father was beyond the various roles he fulfilled.

I also knew his physical and emotional abuse all too well. My disobedience or inability to respond with the appropriate answer was met with harsh and brutal punishment. I grew to intensely fear my father. It was not until I was sixteen years old did I stop trembling in his presence or when he walked into a room that I occupied. I never grew to respect my father as a man or person, except in one area. His work ethic was superb. He always went to work, no matter if it was his full-time or part-time job.

I cannot say that I respected him for being an artist; he never shared this part of his life with me regarding his creative process. Whenever I would notice him working on an art piece, I would ask him about the particular piece he was painting or sculpting. He always responded to my inquiries in a positive way, describing in detail what he was striving to achieve with the brush or his hands. However, he never took the time to share with me what the process of painting or sculpting entailed. One reason why I never paid any attention to my own creativity was the lack of concern displayed in this area by both of my parents.

When I reflect back on the relationship I had with my father, I remember him as a man who struggled with tolerance, forgiveness, understanding, and love. I performed so poorly in grade school and especially in high school. I could never live up to my father's expectations as a student. He thought that I was a "dummy," and I thought that of

Who We Are

myself as well. After my high school graduation ceremonies, during our walk back to the car my father turned to me and said, "I never thought you would make it."

My grades were less than average, and I ranked below the fifty-percent line in my graduating class. I imagine that my father felt justified in making this comment to me based on my below-average performance. Little did I know at that point that I would spend a good portion of my life proving his assessment of me correct. Since *who* I was meant nothing, *what* I was could never matter. It would not be until my sophomore year at Jamestown College that I would experience that I was not a "dummy."

I never knew if my father loved me or not, and to this day I still am not certain of the answer. But I do know today that the answer does not matter. It has no bearing on the fact that I know today that my essence is fundamentally solid and good. There are times, though not often, that I wish I could have known this when my father was still alive. It would have been great to share with him the experience of my redemption. He may have appreciated knowing that one of us was able to break through generations of self-loathing and believing that our essence was *something other than good*.

What We Are

My father passed away on July 13, 1975 from lung cancer. He developed lung cancer as a result of inhaling poisonous fumes from a plastic substance that he was in the process of inventing. My father's art room was upstairs in the back of the house. It was small, and ventilation was extremely poor. The plastic substance was to be used primarily in his sculpting projects. My father was always inventing new techniques to perfect his sculpting and painting. He was superb at his craft. I will always miss this relationship that did not occur.

During my youth, my mother was never able to get beyond using me as an instrument to offset her anger and resentment toward men. I represented for her an opportunity to enact her personal vendetta against the men in her life, which included my father. Her reasons were not obvious to me growing up, but they became apparent to me later on in adulthood. What I came to understand was my mother's unresolved hurt and pain that originated for her in her childhood and adolescence. Her father emotionally, psychologically, physically, and sexually dominated her mother. My grandmother was a woman without her personal authority, autonomy, and dignity in her marriage to my grandfather. As a little boy, whenever my family would visit my grandmother at the Elgin State Hospital, where she lived out her late adulthood, she always appeared forlorn and downhearted.

My mother was to have none of this in her marriage. She would bitterly physically fight my father when they clashed over marital differences. This was her feeble way of letting him know that she was no pushover. She was determined to match him with caustic words and physical strength, but to no avail. Though she realized that she was the "second sex" in the marriage to my father, she was not going to allow him to control her. My mother always felt that men, in general, were not to be trusted, nor were they worthy of experiencing a woman's emotional and sexual vulnerability. She felt that a woman was entitled to withhold her true feelings from the man she was in a primary relationship with, as well as control when she was intimate with him.

My mother was extremely successful at emasculating me during my childhood and early adolescence. She controlled and dominated just about every aspect of my life, except sports. I enjoyed a limited window in which I could experience my masculinity through sports. And

What We Are

when I reached my sixteenth birthday I became more involved in sports, in a dramatic way. If my mother could have, she would have continued to emotionally dominate me well into my adulthood. But when I decided to go away to Jamestown College on a basketball scholarship, this fortunately interrupted her coup. Of course this was against her wishes. She felt that it was my duty to remain at home. It was expected that I help my father and her with the financial responsibilities of the new home our family had just moved into the month I left for school.

Throughout my childhood and adolescence, my mother bought all of my clothes. This meant that she controlled what type of clothing I wore and when I could wear it. She controlled the money I made from my paper routes and part-time jobs as an adolescence. This meant that she could use the money I made for whatever purpose she deemed necessary, and she did. She tightly controlled my time spent outdoors playing. It would not be until my adulthood when I pieced together that on occasions my mother would have my father come after me on the baseball field if I was late for dinner. And he always responded by whipping me back home with his belt or tree limb in full view of my schoolmates.

Who We Are

My mother felt that it was her responsibility to control every aspect of my life and not allow me to have any input. If I questioned or asked why about decisions that directly involved me, she simply would reply, "because I am your mother." I resented my mother for never allowing me to have the opportunity to experience my authority and autonomy. She was unconsciously determined to pass on to me what was denied to her as a child and adolescent. I resented her for never supporting me in personal endeavors that I thought would be good for me. For example, going away to Jamestown College and getting accepted into the University of Chicago's Social Work School, which I later decided against. I went on a three-year drunk instead. My mother wanted me to be emotionally dependent upon her and she came within an eyelash of accomplishing this feat.

I would describe my mother as a great example of a *nice person*. She could be the nicest person you ever would meet. However, if conflict occurred for her, then she could become the meanest person you ever would meet. There is no question in my mind that my mother struggled intensely with an essence that she believed was *something other than good*. I suspect that *something other than good* would be unlovable, not equal to, and undeserving.

What We Are

During the last six or seven years of my mother's life I learned to love her, and I was demonstrative of my love for her. Though she still struggled with her internalized self-loathing, she could allow herself to remain open, if only briefly, to being loved. My gestures of kindness and generosity, which she could tell were genuine, created for both of us moments of deeply felt intimacy. I will never ever forget how I felt reunited with a lost part of myself as a result of being able to love my mother. What helped to make all of this possible was that my mother was mellowing in her senior years; age will have that effect on people.

A contributing factor on my end was that I had moved to Portland, Oregon from Chicago in July, 1983. From 1986 to 1991, much of my own therapy focused on my relationships with women, specifically my mother. My relationships with women were disastrous. I was demanding, controlling, and always acting out the *eternal little boy* who was hoping desperately to be loved. I was able to grieve and grieve deeply the loss of not feeling loved, mothered, and fathered for *who* I was as a child and adolescent.

The process of transitioning out of a belief that my essence was *bad* and *evil* was a very painful one. For me

Who We Are

to experience not feeling loved for *who* I was easily became translated and internalized into feeling that I was unworthy and bad. As I was to later learn, the process of transitioning out of a belief that my essence is *something other than good* was just as painful. What I have come to learn as well, is that it was much easier to accept what I deemed unworthy about myself, but extremely difficult to accept that I was fundamentally good.

I had worked through my resentment and anger toward my mother by the time she started coming to Portland, Oregon to visit in 1990. After she was diagnosed with cancer, our visits with one another were even more precious. Following my move to Seattle, Washington in November 1994, her visits were the greatest experiences I could remember as an adult. I often cried when saying good-bye to her as she would slowly walk down the concourse to board the plane. It would take me two or three days to emotionally recover after her visits.

I experienced great pleasure and joy in accompanying my mother to the University of Washington Medical Center. It was here that she would receive her chemotherapy treatment when visiting. Tears would come to my eyes as we walked the long underground corridor beneath the busy street to get to the entrance of the medical center. For me, it felt like she and I had finally made peace with our relationship; we could finally be together as mother and son. The respect and love that I felt toward her and myself was enormous. I can remember thinking to myself that God had given me the opportunity to finally connect with this woman who was partially responsible for me being in this world. I was determined not to lose this occasion to feel a sense of completeness, at least in this area of my life.

My mother passed away on March 12, 1996 from a heart attack. I remember how shocked I felt when I received the news that she passed away in her sleep. All of my mental and emotional efforts were directed at helping her to fight the cancer. When I heard that it was her heart that failed, I was caught off-guard. Weeks later, when sitting in my car at a local car wash waiting to go through the automatic washing, I watched the planes taking off at the airport, which was only a few miles away. I began crying as I watched the planes climb closer and closer to the heavens and repeated to myself several times, "One day Mom, you and I will be united again." The same experience occurred again the next two visits I made to this particular car wash. I still miss this relationship today.

Who We Are

Both of my parents were selfish and self-centered individuals. I also know that my parents were good people who just did not know this about themselves, either individually or as a couple. They no doubt *fell in love* with each other in the beginning of their relationship, as is customary in our society. What is also customary, which I am certain that my parents experienced, is a belief that this type of love can sustain a relationship and a marriage. But as the marriage developed, neither possessed the emotional tools required to move the marriage to a level where love could be developed based upon a *who* principle.

In other words, they were unable to develop an appreciation for one another based on the essential elements that comprised the essence or basic nature that each embodied. Both had been unsupported and treated as invisible with respect to these solid and good qualities as children and adolescents by their respective adult caretakers. So neither could support nor encourage the other to pursue pathways that would develop *who* they were as individuals. This was why I was not able to have mirrored back to me the qualities that I embodied with respect to my essence being good.

My parents were emotionally and spiritually wounded individuals who had lacked proper mirroring from

What We Are

their adult authority figures in their youth. I feel that I owe my parents a commitment and conviction to reverse a way of life that has been passed from one generation to another. That way of life no longer acceptable is one that would encourage me to believe that my essence and basic nature is *something other than good* or *bad*. I will do whatever it takes to make certain that my mother's life, my father's life, and my life have not been lived in vain.

The dedication in my first book, *RELATIONSHIPS: Shattering The Lies We Live By!*, expresses the gratitude and love I feel today toward my parents. "In memory of my mother, Alpha Jane Howard-Leonard. The first relationship I experienced in this life and the first which taught me compassion. In memory of my father, Lorenzo Robert Leonard. The second relationship I experienced in this life and the first which taught me forgiveness."

Currently, I am listening to the audio version of the *Autobiography of Dr. Martin Luther King, Jr.*, read by LeVar Burton. Time Warner Trade is the publisher and Clayborne Carson is credited with the editing work. Toward the beginning of his story, Dr. King describes growing up in a home filled with love, optimism, and two parents that enjoyed a relationship of compatibility. He mentions how his mother was accessible, and his father—a man of strong will and body—was always involved in the civil rights of African Americans.

Dr. King also describes how his parents prepared him as a young boy to encounter an American way of life that included racism. On a daily basis he would come face to face with a societal system that viewed and treated him as though he was less than and not equal to the white citizen. Fortunately, Dr. King had been taught by his parents how to repel any notion that he was less than and not equal. Most importantly, Dr. King had been taught by his parents that his essence or basic nature was solid and good.

An individual will internalize an essence that is *something other than good* when there is an absence of information mirrored back regarding the intrinsic value and good innately embodied. An individual will internalize an essence that is *bad* or *evil* when there are recurring experiences that remind him or her of being less than or not equal to. Dr. King states in his autobiography, "My mother instilled in all of her children a sense of self-respect from the beginning." He vividly remembers his mother saying to him, "You are as good as anyone." His mother also inspired him to "feel a sense of somebodyness."

What We Are

I do not recall any statements of this nature having been said to me by my parents. Neither do I recall racism, segregation, or discrimination ever being discussed with me by my parents. I attended a racially mixed all-male high school in Chicago, where racism, segregation, and discrimination was present every day. Naïve and unaware is how I would describe myself with respect to the racial problems that I was exposed to at school. During my freshman year, I was expelled from school and "black listed," which meant that I could not enroll in any other Chicago high school. The reason for the drastic measure taken against me was for being involved in a fistfight with a white student.

A white student shoved another African American student and myself out of his way so that he could use a machine during a machine shop class. Harsh words were exchanged between the white and African American student with a promise to finish this altercation after class. The actual fight started between the white and African American student. I began fighting the white student after the African American student was pulled out of the fight by African American upperclassmen. He was badly losing the fight at this point. I was yelled at by African American upperclassmen that if I did not want to be physically beaten by them, then I would have to fight the white student. The fight ended when the teacher of our machine shop class came upon the scene with me in the fistfight with the white student. By this time, everyone had ran away, even the other African American student.

For two full weeks, my parents took turns going to the school to plead with the assistant principal to allow me to return to school, but the emotional pleas were to no avail. The white student and the African American student never had to miss a day of school because of the fight. I was made to be the instigator of the fight, and "this bad apple will be dealt with justly." During this time the white student's parents filed criminal charges against me and were prepared to sue for physical damages. The white student had just completed successful plastic surgery to his face, and there was significant damage to the area of his nose. So my parents and I were interrogated by a detective at the police station in the neighborhood of the school on three separate occasions. My story never changed when told to the assistant principal and the detective; I did not instigate the fight.

At the end of two weeks of frantically trying to get back into any high school, avoid criminal charges, and a

What We Are

personal lawsuit, fate was kind to me. The white student came forward with the truth as to how he had shoved both the other student and myself out of his way. He also admitted to the detective that he did use racially insulting words to further inflict pain on the other student and myself.

The assistant principal, who was white, had dealt with my parents and myself in horribly racist and contemptuous ways. However, fate was not limited to the white student's confession. The assistant principal was suddenly replaced by a new assistant principal at the same time of the confession. Why? I do not know. Fortunately, my parents were able to convince the new assistant principal, who was also white, to allow me to return to school. I was immediately placed on academic probation for the remainder of the school year. This meant that my grade point average could not go below C, or I would be expelled again.

This entire experience with respect to fighting was perplexing and confusing to my parents as well as to me. Up to this point in my life, I would describe myself as passive, weak, and even cowardly. I always avoided physical confrontations. In grade school, my ability to physically protect myself could only be witnessed if my sister or brother was in danger of being taken advantage of by a neighborhood bully. Since I was their older brother, there was an unspoken expectation that I would take up their cause if threatened by someone. Other than that, I felt paralyzed when it came to protecting myself. I would always look for an alley to run down or a building to duck into if I was physically threatened. As an adult, I would come to understand how my lack of courage was a result of my emasculation.

When I became involved in this fistfight, not yet two months into the school year, I was way out of character. However, I dared not let the students know this information about myself or I would be in plenty of trouble. I deathly feared being routinely picked on by school bullies if they knew just how fearful and passive I felt internally. A curious dynamic had occurred for me, which lasted throughout my years in high school, and one that I could build upon as well. I had gained a reputation. I went up against a white student, the school power structures, was punished, and I returned to tell the tale.

My initiation into the *club of toughness* had been a successful one. When my brother entered the same high school two years later, word would circulate, "Don't mess with Eric, he is Lorenzo's brother." As I look back on this

What We Are

period in my life, I realize how I stumbled into a reputation of being tough. This awkward transition permitted me to effectively hide from others and myself an area of deep emotional wounding. I was an adolescent male who did not possess a strong sense of my masculinity. Little did I know at this time that I would have a number of experiences during my adolescence that would further perpetuate a lie with respect to *who* I was. The lie was that I was *macho* and fearless.

In contrast, it goes without saying that I was a total disappointment and a major source of frustration to my parents. After getting back into school, I believe it was a month before either one of them spoke to me in more than one or two sentences. I was well on my way to setting the stage for my father to say to me on graduation night, "I never thought that you would make it."

Relations between the African American and white students were always tense. We just stayed out of each other's way and we both understood where each one's territory began and ended. I learned to respect the white students' power and influence, always treading lightly when the boundaries seemed vague. For instance, when buying sweet rolls at the local bakery, it was important not to cut in front of a white student if in doubt who was the next buyer. All that the African American students wanted was complete control over the fringes. Basketball and football were the fringes that belonged to the African American student. Still and all, my self-perception and essence remained less than and not equal to.

Dr. King's exemplary life as a Baptist minister and civil rights leader will forever remain with me as an example of the model of cooperation put into action. What he accomplished for the advancement of an individual's personal essence and dignity, bathed in good, will remain as one of this country's designated periods of enlightenment. Dr. King helped to raise the level of awareness for all people with respect to equality, integrity, and accountability. I, too, had experienced a wave of enthusiasm that maybe, just maybe, I was indeed *somebody* who was equal to, possessed integrity, and could be accountable for my behavior.

This same acknowledgement can be said of Malcolm X as well. Both men had experienced widespread philosophical disagreement, even between each other, with respect to their particular ideologies. Still, each man was able to push the American culture to examine itself concerning our racial attitudes and practices. Dr. King and

What We Are

Malcolm X could rightfully claim that it was their essence, founded in good, that spearheaded this shift in the psychology of our society. We began to understand some of the emotional and behavioral characteristics of one another relative to ethnicity. And a significant part of that psychology included the racial attitudes and practices embedded in American culture.

I reference Malcolm X in the above paragraph because I could not in good conscious mention Dr. King's impact on the American culture without briefly citing his impact as well. Both, in my estimation, will go down in African American and American history as contributors to enacting a model of cooperation that millions throughout the world felt compelled to follow.

Though we witnessed a shift in the psychology of American society, this shift was not permanent. For many African Americans and whites, indignity and contemptuous behavior towards one another shifted momentarily in favor of liberalism and skepticism. This was not a uniform condition, because there were instances on both sides where the shift was made with a degree of sincerity. But, for the majority of Americans involved in the civil rights movement, this period of enlightenment was short-lived.

Who We Are

We only need to look at the racial tension and polarity that exist today to confirm this observation.

Nevertheless, this change in racial attitudes and practices was not to last long beyond Dr. King's eulogy and burial. The problem was that this shift in behavior for many African and white Americans was a result of living vicariously through its leader, Dr. King. Change of this nature could not become permanent because it was not emanating from within the individual followers of the civil rights movement. A shift in behavior was being made on a group level, rather than individually. Because Dr. King exemplified the principles he taught and spoke for the masses, this was quite enough for many of his followers. His followers could allow him to push for an agenda that they were not ready to transition into, an essence that was fundamentally sound and good.

For disdainful behavior, racial or otherwise, to be replaced by respectful behavior on a permanent basis, an individual will necessarily experience a personal confrontation. This confrontation is between the essence of the individual, which is based in good, and the lie an individual has internalized with respect to his or her essence. The lie represents a culmination of experiences that negatively reinforce that an individual's essence or basic nature is *not* fundamentally good.

For example, not being informed of personal attributes that are good and positive nor encouraged to experience them in one's life. The lie that is created in place of the truth, as far as one's essence not being good, usually takes shape in one of three forms. One's essence is believed to be either *something other than good, bad,* or *evil.*

This deep personal confrontation with self will oftentimes unearth emotional pain, such as anguish and grave disappointment. It is easier to believe the lie about one's essence than to acknowledge, accept, and live the truth that one is fundamentally good. We have spent considerably more time living and perpetuating the lie than we have perpetuating and promoting the truth about self. So the confrontation will not be an easy one, but it will reveal the truth about one's self. This truth is the absolute good that an individual is anchored in, despite not being loved, appreciated, or educated about one's finest qualities from individuals who have been entrusted with one's well-being.

An individual determines that unethical behavior misrepresents his or her essence or basic nature, which is firmly affixed in good. Behavior that does not demonstrate emotional integrity, personal dignity, and accountability is rejected because of an undeniable acceptance that one's essence is fundamentally good. This shift in behavior, in order to become permanent, emerges from within the individual and not through an identification with a leader, group, or community.

There are individuals who will state that this is exactly the process that he or she encountered as they were becoming part of Dr. King's civil rights movement. There is little doubt that many individuals actually believed that they were moving through this process of self-examination as they were holding hands in defiance of racial injustice. However, what that process of self-examination lacked was the acknowledgement and reversal of an essence they initially believed to be *something other than good.*

How can I make this accusation? Easily. If this level of self-examination had occurred for those that found merit in Dr. King's message, they would have followed him not only in principle but in practice as well. Millions of affected people simply would not have chosen to vicariously live through Dr. King. The change in racial attitudes and practices would have lasted far beyond Dr. King's death. The

What We Are

shift that we experienced at that time would still be with us today. It would have been a permanent change. But, because change was not experienced on an individual level first, Dr. King's idea of racial and social equality was allowed to die with him. Not many of his followers had made their own personal journey reversing an essence that was originally believed to be *something other than good*.

Respect, love, and integrity cannot be experienced in primary and secondary relationships on a genuine basis until one's own essence is first acknowledged, accepted, and lived as being fundamentally solid and good. We will never have the experience before the transformation. Dr. King's dream of racial and social equality died with him because a significant number of individuals who comprised the movement were not able to make this personal leap.

The group effort can never replace individual redemption. If an individual is to know that he or she is *somebody*, then an emotional and spiritual transition out of a *nobody* place will become a necessary personal journey to incur. Dr. King knew that he was *somebody* because he had parents that made certain that he knew that his essence or basic nature was basically solid and good. Dr. King's parents made certain that their son began his life journey

Who We Are

in this fashion. So the movement that Dr. King started with all the good intentions quickly collapsed upon his death.

Collectively speaking, the African American experienced an elevated sense of self that manifested itself primarily through a group effort. Suddenly African Americans were brothers and sisters with pride, confidence, and a "somebodyness" that Dr. King initially described as one of his mother's teachings. African Americans were joining hands together unlike any time in our recorded history. Not since World War II, when African American soldiers were in Europe as part of the war machine, had there been such a group excitement generated.

As a society, we were able to confront issues of domination like we never had before in this country. Whites and African Americans alike, were challenging voting privileges, segregation, and racial injustices relative to housing, educational, and employment practices. There were as many white citizens as African Americans who assembled together to change a historical American way of life steeped in injustice. These courageous individuals were hoping to replace a model of racial, political, educational, and economic domination with one of cooperation.

What We Are

When Dr. King was suddenly taken from us, because we, as a society, had not made this journey on an individual basis, much of what this man taught and preached literally vaporized. As a society, we have unfortunately regressed to alarming depths of apathy and self-indulgence since Dr. King's passing. Virtues such as personal integrity, dignity, accountability, and a sense of community are in danger of being relegated to levels of unimportance.

Self-indulgence is everywhere. Very little interest is expressed today concerning genuine efforts to live in relationships and a society that is cohesive. African Americans are no longer brothers and sisters; we hardly ever speak to one another when passing on the streets or riding public transportation. This was a significant contemporary trademark of our solidarity. Instead, we have become more distrustful of one another, which has been our historical trademark.

Granted, a few African Americans have made tremendous strides economically in the area of sports. However, outside of the sports arena, a majority of African Americans continue to struggle to gain access to mainstream America. In addition to this, the white culture has returned

Who We Are

with a vengeance to become obsessed with its own well-being. For example, the elimination of Affirmative Action programs. Working ever so hard to maintain the status quo, the white culture remains the dominant culture in every phase of the word.

During the past four years, I have been thoroughly involved in a process of writing. I now understand its purpose to be the resurgence of *who* I am as a worthy, contributory, and loving individual. Writing has allowed me to experience my essence and basic nature as being essentially solid and good. During this same time period, I have been involved in countless discussions with friends, relatives, and clients. The focus has been on the importance of writing to enhance the quality of relationships involving self and others.

The style of writing that I am proposing reawakens an individual to the fact that his or her essence and basic nature is fundamentally solid and good. And as a result of this reawakening, a discovery that primary and secondary relationships are enhanced as well. The framework for this style of writing is one of self-examination. It is primarily comprised of accountability, compassion, and redemption.

What We Are

This format encourages a person to examine an essence or basic nature that he or she believes is *something other than good, bad,* or *evil*.

This format also encourages an individual to relive experiences that contributed to establishing or reinforcing this negative self-perception. The experiences in question are behaviors of indignity directed towards others, directed towards self by others and acts of indignity against one's self by self. Accountability assumes four significant roles throughout this entire process.

First, there is the opportunity to relive an incident or series of incidents to discern and give credibility to the emotions and feelings that may have occurred. In some situations, a person will either deny and repress the feelings or simply not know what he or she was feeling during a particular incident. Experiences of this nature usually were too painful to remain emotionally present. Accountability provides a person with the opportunity to claim or reclaim ownership of his or her feelings. As we already know, this is an invaluable component to one's experiences.

Second, accountability provides an opportunity to look at one's self during the incident or series of incidents.

Who We Are

This can be helpful when reliving experiences of indignity when a person is the recipient of this behavior. This introspective view allows an individual to correctly re-evaluate any experience that resulted in shame and reproach from an objective vantage point. Presumably, a negative self-perception had previously been internally established, which would usually stem from internalizing earlier experiences that resulted in shame and indignity.

Thus, a safe assumption can be made that the previous incident or series of incidents were experienced from a subjective position. That is, the experience or experiences of shame and reproach were originally perceived as a personal affront. For a child, adolescent, and young adult, this would be a natural response to conclude. When there is little to no awareness of personal autonomy and personal good, it is easy to perceive experiences of shame and reproach as a personal affront, especially when there is the absence of a *somebodyness*.

The same approach is used for indignity and shame-based behavior directed toward others and toward one's self. Accountability provides an opportunity to examine one's self and take responsibility for injuring others, including self. The reflective view allows a person to

What We Are

correctly re-evaluate the incident or incidents as acting from a place of depravation. The belief that one's essence or basic nature is *something other than good*, *bad*, or *evil* can now begin to be reversed. One effective way to take responsibility for destructive behavior is to enact the truth about one's self: *somebodyness* with an essence that is assuredly good.

In retrospect, this is what Dr. Martin Luther King, Jr. enjoyed as a little boy growing up in his home. He had parents who taught him, and taught him well, that he was indeed somebody. Somebody because of what he personally embodied: compassion, autonomy, dignity, personal authority, emotional integrity, and value as a human being. I say again, the civil rights movement collapsed after Dr. King's untimely death for one specific reason. Many of its followers, on an individual basis, had failed to transition out of a belief that their respective essence was *something other than good, bad,* or *evil.* What remained unacknowledged was knowing that their essence was unmistakably *good.*

Third, accountability provides a person with the opportunity to experience the statement made at the end of the previous paragraph. That being, to transition out of an essence that is believed to be *something other than good, bad*, or *evil* and into knowing that one's essence is good. The measuring stick that will always determine where an individual positions himself or herself regarding this difference will be internal and external conflict.

Will there be an emotional and spiritual spiraling downward? In other words, will the individual feel a sense of unworthiness, less than, or not equal to as a reaction to the conflict? This will be evidenced by a need to use cruelty, violence, condemnation, demonization, or degrading judgement against others as well as one's self. Or, there will be an ability to face conflict in its fullness without resorting to debasing behavior. And just as important, while facing conflict in its fullness, there will be the ability to protect the dignity and integrity of self and others.

And here is where the work actually takes on a fierce challenge. With respect to being the recipient of shame-based behavior, the following would apply. In some situations, the incident or series of incidents resulting in humiliation and reproach were indeed meant to be taken as a personal affront. For example, when racism and sexism are directed at a person. However, it is imperative to know at this point that no matter what occurred during the

What We Are

experiences resulting in shame and reproach, one truth remained unblemished. The essence or basic nature was not diminished at all.

This statement also applies to the transgressor who perpetrates debasing behavior on another individual, including one's self. It matters not with respect to how degrading and shame-based the injury, or whether the nature of the injury is emotional, psychological, spiritual, or physical. The experience or experiences will never touch nor harm the core of *who* an individual is with regards to one's essence and basic nature. No individual will ever be so powerful as to accomplishing this endeavor, though our history as a nation is replete with many who have tried.

Admittedly so, the practice of domination relentlessly seeks to convey the opposite. However, it simply cannot diminish an individual's essence or basic nature when it is firmly affixed to what is good within that individual. It is merely an exercise in futility. The effectiveness of any form of domination is determined by either an implied or expressed consent to be victimized.

Once more, this statement would apply to the transgressor. The transgressor agrees by either expressed or implied consent to engage in the practice of domination. This person will injure another and self because of a perceived damage to his or her essence by those adhering to the practice of domination in that person's life. Thus, this individual has internalized a deep sense of victimization. And when an individual consents to be victimized, it is because there is little or no sense of one's essence being unmistakably solid and good.

Yes, there are situations that arise in which a person is a victim of another person's indignity. However, this person consents to internalize the experience to such a degree that his or her essence is diminished. This is why most injuries enacted against an individual's essence and basic nature occur during childhood and adolescence. At this age, there is little or no sense of one's essence being unmistakably sound and good. This is not to say that injuries directed at the essence and basic nature of an adult do not occur. To the contrary, our history as a society is replete with acts of indignity directed at adults by adults. However, the impact of these injustices would be greatly minimized if not for the internalization of the acts of indignity that occurred during childhood and adolescence.

When inflicting indignity and shame-based behavior upon another individual or one's self, it is important to

What We Are

remember one fact. The intent behind it is to reinforce the lie that one's own essence and basic nature is *something other than good, bad, or evil*. A transgressor may want to think otherwise. Nonetheless, the underlying motivation for perpetrating debasing behavior onto another person or one's self remains constant. Over and again, the intent is to remain married to a belief that one's essence and basic nature is *something other than good, bad, or evil*.

Since another person's essence cannot be impacted by degrading behavior, except by expressed or implied consent, the objective is simple. The objective is to locate that person or persons who will consent either overtly or covertly to being victimized. Indignity ceases when there is no victimization to go along with the victim. And when there is victimization, the transgressor has been successful in finding a person who believes his or her essence is *something other than good, bad, or evil*. The old saying, "misery loves company," certainly applies here.

It is during this third stage of accountability that one's writings begin to express compassion and redemption. To transition out of a belief that one's essence is *something other than good, bad, or evil* and into knowing that one's essence is good, requires conviction and courage. Writing about experiences that resulted in shame and reproach without adding compassion and redemption is merely journal recording. And the best that journal writing can offer an individual is temporary relief from internal anguish.

If this entire process is to have value and meaning, then compassion for one's suffering and redemption for that suffering will be incorporated into the writings. That is, making declarations of forgiveness to one's self for having turned against one's true essence and basic nature; admitting that this occurred because the incident or incidents that resulted in shame and reproach led to a sense of there being something wrong with the individual. A sense of oneness enters an individual's heart after declaring forgiveness and allowing compassion to filter into each shame-based episode. Atonement is redemption. It emerges when a person is prepared to stop embracing experiences that support the belief that one's essence is *something other than good, bad,* or *evil.*

The process is identical with respect to acknowledging compassion for that person or persons, including self, adversely impacted by one's degrading behavior. Declarations of forgiveness to those individuals, including one's self, that were harmed by the destructive behavior are absolutely necessary if this entire process is to act as a cleansing experience. Again, an individual must forgive

What We Are

himself or herself for having turned against one's true essence and basic nature, which is rooted in good. As a result of being emotionally dominated during childhood and adolescence, an adult will often seek to dominate others in a similar manner. This would be an excellent example of turning against one's true essence.

The steps described thus far for this style of writing are intended to accomplish one definite objective: securing the emotional and spiritual footsteps that necessitate transiting into knowing that one's essence and basic nature is irrevocably good. The healing agents for any type of wound that results from the practice of domination are compassion and redemption. Separating from internalizing a shame-based experience as a personal affront and merging these healing agents into one's writings will assure that this occurs. Humility becomes the inner garment that gracefully testifies to the transition into an essence that is undeniably good. It replaces arrogance. It is a trademark for individuals who have the courage to establish a way of life based on *who* they are, rather than *what* they are.

The fourth step involves consolidating this writing exercise into a format that can be shared or read by another person. Not that it is necessary to share this exercise with a close friend or support group, or that it is a requirement that they read this document. But it is an excellent idea to prepare this writing as though it will be shared or read by another individual. To experience the willingness to extend one's self can help immensely in rendezvousing with an essence that is good. This step also involves encouraging the writer to enlarge upon his or her personal scope. For example, indicating through one's writings how other men, women, or children may benefit from this new information and insight. Principally, how others may be impacted by this or similar experiences that resulted from a practice of domination.

Consolidating one's writing into this type of format can be enormously rewarding and liberating. Experiencing the pinnacle and clarity of one's intelligence and genius is the most effective way to reverse the repugnant effects of domination. This is especially true since one primary motivation is to remind the transgressor and the victims that his or her intelligence is limited or insufficient. The practice of domination, regardless if one is the transgressor or the victim, seeks to reduce an individual's intelligence and spirit to its lowest ebb, that is, nonexistent.

The aim at this stage of the writing process is to encourage the writer to express with clarity new information

What We Are

and insight. Precisely, new information and insight he or she has learned about self as a result of this in-depth personal examination. The new awareness and understanding regarding one's self represents the undeniable truth that an individual's essence is indeed good. This is a result of facing past and present experiences relative to the practice of domination. It is also a result of understanding how the adverse effects from this practice were adopted to establish or reinforce a belief that one's essence is *something other than good, bad,* or *evil.*

This final step is a significant one. It allows the writer to elaborate on the process of transiting into knowing that his or her essence is good. It also allows the writer to contribute to the enhancement of another individual. This is an important step because it is the beginning of giving to another based on *who* one is intrinsically, rather than *what* one is externally. Once more, it is not the goal of this particular process to write a book or an article for publication. Though an individual may seek to make this his or her personal endeavor, it is not an objective of this exercise. The end result is not what matters here; the process itself is the goal.

Writing to experience the pinnacle of one's intelligence and with a *spirit* to share this gift that will help improve the life of others is what matters. Overcoming the practice of domination by knowing that one's essence is good will always occur on a personal level first, if this new way of living is to have value. The writer will choose where to go with his or her gift as this experience becomes a permanent basis in which to reside. Adding to the lives of others in a life-enhancing manner, one that emanates from *who* one is, can personally elevate both the beneficiary and the writer.

The utmost value and contributory potential that a person innately possesses, devoid of any external role, can only be exceeded by an accumulation of these experiences. Contributory in the sense of being able to enhance not only one's life, but the lives of others as a direct result of expressing an essence that is good. Contributory because of a universal truth, which is acting as the guardian, not only of one's own dignity and emotional integrity, but that of another's as well.

My goal, during this stage in my life, is to establish a way of life in which I can experience dignity and emotional integrity, first with myself and then in my relationships. This book serves as an example of the writing process I have just described. My desire in writing this book was to keep in stride with the powerful words of the English poet,

What We Are

Cecil Day-Lewis. He eloquently stated, "We do not write in order to be understood, we write in order to understand."

I chose to publish this book because I wanted to share what I have learned concerning the practice of domination and how domination has impacted my life. I know that if I am adversely impacted by the practice of domination with respect to my essence, so are others, regardless of class, gender, and race. I share my insights because I also know that the essence of each and every person who comprises our world community to be undeniably good.

Reawakening to an essence or basic nature that is fundamentally good is a natural consequence of first being open to self-examination. This particular process of writing allows an individual to reestablish the fact that he or she was born with an essence and basic nature that was good. Writing with this style in mind effectively confronts any personal issue that arises from the emotional, physical, and spiritual impact concerning the practice of domination.

Yes, this is a painful process, and not an easy one to accomplish. This is an emotional and spiritual growth process that requires personal discipline and conviction in order to achieve success. But this is what establishing trust and credibility with one's self is built upon: confirming one's experiences with accountability, compassion, and redemption. The overall intent of these writings is to mirror back to an individual invaluable information about one's self. In particular, information that will lead to knowing that *who* an individual is on an innate level is basically good. Establishing credibility for one's experiences and feelings without condemnation, blame, demonization, or cruelty allows for personal authority, autonomy, and legitimacy to take root internally.

In looking back, a number of my discussions regarding the benefits of writing, actually began prior to my own personal experiences with it. Later, as I began writing my books, the discussions became more intense with respect to my encouragement to clients, friends, and relatives to write. However, I still had not arrived at fully comprehending on a conscious level to what degree I was being impacted by my writing experiences. Nevertheless, I knew that the experience would benefit anyone who dared to undertake the endeavor.

During these early discussions and prior to my writing experiences, I strongly believed that the experience of writing would provide an opportunity for an individual to

What We Are

experience his or her inherent authority, autonomy, and personal legitimacy. And what I am referring to by personal legitimacy is the ultimate value and contributory capacity an individual inherently possesses, which is devoid of external roles. Contributory in the sense of being able to enhance not only one's life, but the lives of others as a direct result of expressing an essence that is good.

What I did not fully understand during the early conversations was the overall impact that an individual would be exposed to as a result of this experience. My understanding lacked the realization that writing would actually reawaken an individual to his or her essence or basic nature as inherently sound and good. I was not consciously aware of this crucial piece of enlightenment until I was mid-way through collaborating on the book, *Made From Scratch*.

Four years ago, on an unconscious level, I more than likely knew that the experience of writing would have the power to restore to its original form an essence that was once believed to be damaged. But as I continued to ponder this unconscious phenomenon, I realized that I did in fact know about the benefits of writing since my junior year at Jamestown College. It was then, in 1968,

Who We Are

that I began writing my first book, *Once Upon A Time and Other Poems*. After I graduated, I then moved to San Jose, California and continued to write. During the middle of 1971, I moved back to Chicago, and continued to write my book until it was finished in 1972.

I was fortunate to find a local press that would extend their resources to help me transform my manuscript into a book. I recall meeting with a representative from this particular company one cool, crisp fall afternoon in downtown Chicago. The representative expressed his delight with the book and thought it best that we use the above-mentioned title, rather than the title I had originally chosen. To this day I cannot remember what I originally titled the book. The representative followed this up with book production ideas and extensive marketing strategies. Needless to say, I was thrilled and nervous about the prospect of publishing my thoughts and feelings on the subject of being a black man living in America. This book was a product of the late 1960s. It was a period of time when everybody had something to say about everything, and that included me. However, before I could make a decision to go forward with this project, I felt the necessity to share my book and plans with my parents.

What We Are

Before launching into that experience, I will provide some backdrop information to help understand the complete picture. By the time I graduated from college in May 1969, approximately one hundred fellow students had read what I had written up to that point. And by the time I left the San Jose area in 1971, another one hundred or so assortment of coworkers and friends had read it. When I completed the manuscript in 1972, a rough estimate of three hundred people had either read the manuscript in segments or in its entirety. I describe the incident in this manner to emphasize that my mother and father represented roughly the 301st and 302nd persons, respectively, who read the manuscript.

I had arranged for them to read the manuscript separately on a Friday evening in their home. I first gave the manuscript to my mother. She returned to the kitchen, where I had been nervously awaiting her response, in an hour's time. My mother was very positive and supportive with her response to my book. She said that she had enjoyed reading it. She wanted to know what inspired me to write this book and she encouraged me to follow through with my plans to publish it. I can't tell you how excited I felt; I was beyond words that would adequately describe my joy. This was the first time in my life that my mother expressed to me positive words and encouraging statements for undertaking an endeavor that was my own idea.

With my chest out and feeling quite confident, I then gave the manuscript to my father. For the first time, I felt proud of what I had written and I now anticipated hearing my father's words of surprise and encouragement. In less than an hour, he was down from his upstairs bedroom with the manuscript in his right hand. The look on his face signaled to me that disapproval of some sort was on the horizon, but I held onto the hope that I had misread his facial expression. Unfortunately for me, I was proven wrong.

My father was quick to the point. He did not like the manuscript and he certainly would not support nor encourage me to publish the manuscript in book form. He said that the manuscript was too revealing with respect to my thoughts and feelings. I would be giving people information to use against me, if they chose to do so. I responded to him by saying, "I am simply writing about my experiences as a black man living in this country. And I am using prose and poetry as my framework, what is wrong with that? At any rate, who would want to hurt me, and why?"

He merely handed me the manuscript and stated that it was not a good idea. My father then turned and walked back up the stairs and into his art room. He and I never exchanged more than five or six sentences between one another for the remaining years of his life. When my father passed away, I felt my heart break. I knew that I still had so much to say to him. On the day of his funeral, I laid in a drunken stupor, cursing and damning any and all family members. My heart wrenches with great remorse and sorrow as I recall these distressing moments.

I did not feel devastated by his rationale for me to not publish the book. What I felt devastated by was the emphatic *no* that he did not like what I had written. I felt deeply hurt that he thought the idea of publishing the book was a bad one. I could never sleep, drug, or drink away the pain of my father's emphatic *no*. So desperate was I to impress this man with my ability to think and write, that I now felt unbelievably depressed. To have my father think differently of me from what he stated on that ominous night of my high school graduation would have been ecstatic. In my mind, I was yet another disappointment to him. And in some ways, I still feel the hint of this even though I know it is not a reality. He was roughly the 302nd person to read the manuscript and the only person to tell me that it was not good.

Who We Are

Regretfully so, I often found myself years later wishing that my father could have disagreed with the content but still supported my efforts to publish the manuscript. I subsequently destroyed the manuscript, leaving the last remaining copy with a drug and alcohol counselor. I entered drug and alcohol treatment, for the first time, in the summer of 1976. As part of providing a personal history, I disclosed to one of the counselors that I had written a manuscript for book publication. He asked to read the manuscript, and I felt extremely elated. After a few days, the counselor informed me that he enjoyed reading my perspectives regarding being a black man living in America. His response to my manuscript gave me a temporary reprieve from my internalized self-hatred. I just wanted to hear from him that I was a good writer.

Many years later, I was to learn that I was writing neither to be understood nor to understand. I had solely written this first book in order to be validated and approved of as a good person. Somehow, I had translated that if I were a good writer, then I would be considered a good person. Neither experience was to occur for me until many years later, and for reasons that were more authentic. By the way, my alcoholism and drug addiction had nothing to do with my parents. This was just another way to plunge

What We Are

myself further down the emotional and spiritual ladder of despair. Alcohol and drugs were used as vehicles to transition into believing that my essence and basic nature was indeed *bad*.

What my father exposed for me on that dreadful Friday evening was just how deficient I was in the area of my self-worth. The depth to which the belief that my essence was *something other than good* ran very deep within me, and it was pervasive. Over three hundred people had read my manuscript and responded in a positive way. Yet because he, being my father, had found the manuscript unacceptable, I chose to descend into a downward emotional and spiritual spiral. I felt unworthy and undeserving of another person's love and I felt incapable of loving. The rejection of my work had been translated as a rejection of me on a deep personal level.

Yes, my father and mother were responsible for laying the foundation concerning my emotional and spiritual deficiency. Could I blame them for this deficiency? Could I resent them for laying the groundwork that my essence and basic nature was *something other than good*? And could I hate them for teaching me as a child and adolescent to embody this lie about myself that was routinely confirmed by my experiences with them?

Who We Are

Grievously for me, I did blame, resent, and hate my mother and father for all of the above reasons. And I can say, without hesitation, that it was a waste of my time and of my life. To hold my parents as hostages for passing on to me what they, individually and collectively, were so unaware of was absurd. It was natural to feel hurt and angry with respect to how I was raised by my parents. But I would not learn this valuable piece of information until well into my adulthood.

They, too, individually and collectively, embodied an essence and basic nature that was believed to be *something other than good*. Each possessed a blind eye and a deaf ear to this knowledge and each suffered unnecessarily from its effects. Both my mother and father knew on an individual and collective level that all was not emotionally and spiritually right within; this was why each was committed to the practice of domination as a way of life. When there is an absence of knowing that one's essence is good, the practice of domination will fill this inner vacuum.

Tragically, no adult figures in their respective childhood and adolescent years had ever stopped long enough to teach either my mother or my father about the undeniable good of their personal essence. These were the conditions

What We Are

under which my parents lived during their youth. The same conditions can be safely assumed regarding their grandparents and great-grandparents. My family legacy is one in which no one was educated to the truth that his or her very essence and basic nature was irrevocably good. If this were not true, then the smallest hint of being accepted for *who* I am would have surfaced somewhere in my experiences with my parents.

Causes are irrelevant and meaningless. Blaming, resenting, and hating my parents never brought to a positive conclusion my acceptance of the lie that my essence and basic nature *was something other than good* and *bad*. As a matter of fact, the longer I maintained one or more of these rigid stances, the more I perpetuated this negative self-perception. I believe that the sins of the father and mother will be visited upon the children. I also believe that the acceptance of an individual's good should be made manifest in order to rid the effects of the father and mother's sins. Moreover, to rid the sin of defining the father and mother's sins as sin.

If an individual is not consciously and deliberately taught that his or her essence and basic nature is inherently good, then one conclusion will be certain to occur. That being, *who* that individual innately is will be deemed

Who We Are

irrelevant by him or her. And thus the stage is set to perpetuate the practice of domination as a basis for relationships to exist. Without the basic knowledge that one is irrevocably good, a person will arm him or herself with the weapons of domination: power, intimidation, and manipulation.

In general, it is difficult for men and women to accept a personal essence and basic nature that is good when there is a history and current practice of domination with respect to one another—sexism. In general, it is difficult for whites and blacks to accept a personal essence and basic nature that is good, when there is a history and current practice of domination with respect to one another—racism. Generally speaking, it is difficult for women to accept one another as possessing an essence and basic nature that is good, when there is a history and current practice of domination among themselves—internalized sexism. Generally speaking, it is difficult for African Americans to accept one another as possessing an essence and basic nature that is good, where there is a history and current practice of domination among themselves—internalized racism.

These are but a few examples of how the practice of domination resides within our society. Each group dominates another and themselves in different ways, but for the same reasons: power and control. Neither can accept the basic truth relative to possessing an innate essence and basic nature that is, without fail, absolutely good. I firmly believe that the root cause for our personal maladies and societal ills is due to this issue of essence. The root causes for violence, cruelty, and prejudice, hence the practice of domination, is the internalized belief that one's essence is *something other than good, bad,* or *evil.*

CONCLUSION

What We Are

*"You can take anything,
no matter how good you treat it,
...it wants to be free.
You can treat it good, and feed it good, and give it
everything it seems to want.
But, if you open the cage, it's happy."*

Tom Robinson, former North Carolina slave

There is little doubt that Mr. Robinson was speaking in terms of slavery and the African American slave. As to the correctness of Mr. Robinson's statement with regard to an individual's desire for personal freedom, I would assume that there would be total agreement as well. I am impressed with this prophetic statement because it can be expanded upon to include a significant aspect of the American way of life that we, individually and collectively, have established for ourselves. The American way of life with respect to how we excuse ourselves from proper acknowledgement and development of personal essence can be paralleled with Mr. Robinson's last sentence, "But, if you open the cage, it's happy."

Who We Are

Since its inception, our way of life has consistently and relentlessly come under close analysis from all corners of the world, which include every possible persuasion inside its borders. From top to bottom, inside and out, every aspect of our way of life has been closely examined and critiqued. I have discovered in recent years one glaring fact as a result of reading and listening to a wide range of thoughts and opinions regarding our social, political, economic, and religious ways of life. What will frequently influence an individual's point of view as well as his or her suggestions for improvement, is the ideology he or she embraces with respect to a political right, left, or middle.

The political dictionary located at www.fasttimes.com provides an excellent definition for these terms. "Political right is on the far conservative side of the political spectrum. Its politics usually favor a free enterprise system in which business is unfettered by government regulation, a strong military, not much spending on social services, and a tough stance on crime. The political left advocates generous spending on the welfare state, vigorously promotes the rights of women and minorities, is suspicious of high spending on defense, tends to be internationalist in outlook, favors government controls on the free market system, and generally favors social welfare over business interests.

What We Are

Moderate political policies are those that occupy the middle ground between the right and the left and that do not try to effect fundamental social change."

Regardless of how strong an individual is affiliated with one political ideology or another, few thoughts and opinions are expressed that are not heavily influenced by this political affiliation. Thoughts, opinions, and actions that would advance or enhance all American citizens, regardless of race, religion, class, or gender are severely compromised by this particular alliance. A major cause for this compromise is the inability to separate one's political persuasion from a loyalty that each individual comprising our society is linked to and mutually shares, whether recognized or not. That loyalty in which we mutually share with one another is, acting as the guardian of one another's dignity and integrity.

Regardless of race, religion, class, or gender differences, because we are linked together as one common humanity, we are to *safeguard* each other's nobility of character. Protecting one another against experiences that would demean and debase an individual is what I am referring to by the term safeguard. Another way in which the term can be viewed would be the ability to champion

Who We Are

one's own and another individual's dignity. A reader may respond to this by stating, "Hello, this is the twenty-first century, wake up! Who has time to be concerned with such matters that do not involve me?" True, this is the twenty-first century. However, I do remain troubled by an overall inability of people to take into serious consideration each American citizen in the endeavor to improve as a whole the American way of life. And this would include protecting the nobility and integrity of all Americans, regardless of their social, political, legal, and economic status.

To some, this may seem naïve and unrealistic. However, if we as a society are to push forward with a serious agenda to combat the divisions that violence, cruelty, greed, and power are threatening our basic survival with today, then this way of life becomes a priority. As a society, we simply cannot continue to be threatened on a daily basis by these issues. There is a direct link between the increased violence and cruelty that we are experiencing and a lack of acceptance and recognition regarding the essential good of an individual's essence and basic nature.

As a society, we cannot continue to support a way of life constructed around fear and distrust and hope to sustain some semblance of cohesiveness. This I do profess

What We Are

to know, that if an individual accepts his or her essence and basic nature as undeniably good, then that individual will not stop short of being the guardian of another individual's dignity and integrity. That individual will not allow personal ideology to separate him or her from helping to make certain that every citizen in our society has an equal opportunity to experience the freedom to be *who* he or she is innately.

The American way of life, in its entirety, is full of great potential. If it is allowed to function with its stated purpose and all of its citizens in mind, this potential can develop into a personal freedom that every inhabitant can enjoy. Rather than continue promoting an abstract concept for a freedom that we profess to live, let us honor that shared loyalty that binds us as a humanity. It is our individual and collective responsibility to bring forth our personal good and to assist one another in the same endeavor. And we can, without fail, accomplish this feat by accepting and recognizing how vital it is to live one's life based on *who* that individual is, simply because it is based in good.

It is my intention to offer new insights regarding the importance of inserting into our way of life an essence and basic nature that is fundamentally good and based on the intrinsic value of an individual. The most effective way to accomplish this task, in my opinion, is through the writing exercise that I discussed in part two of this book. I know that once we can institute this change on a personal level, it will immediately decrease the need for violence, cruelty, condemnation, and destructive behavior that is gripping our society today. Politically, I align myself with neither the political right, left, or middle. Though my books could lead the reader to assume that I align myself with the political left, this is further from the truth. It is true that I am a strong advocate for social change, but this social change is for our society as a whole, and not just for a few select groups.

I do stand as a representative of a way of life that would promote and put into action a model of cooperation, rather than the current model of domination that is used by our society. I also stand as a representative of a way of life that is totally committed to preserving the dignity and integrity of each individual comprising our society. I do not stand as a representative of a political, economical, or social agenda that would continue to preserve a way of life that usurps the dignity and integrity of an individual. And to my way of thinking, the political right, left, and middle, as observed in our current political, economic, and social arenas, continues to do so.

What We Are

The American way of life, at first glance, can look like the popular magician, David Copperfield at his best, creating a wonderful world of magic and illusion. The appearance that there are no strings or props positioning the acts have his audiences believing in a freedom that exists only in the minds of the naïve. In a significant way, such is the American way of life. With so much emphasis appointed to being nice rather than the personal conviction to live from a place of good, the illusion that is created by this behavior is that we are a society mainly comprised of people who know that they are basically good. This unfortunately is not true. I personally know that we are a society mainly comprised of good and caring people. However, the problem that has consistently existed, not just in our society but throughout the world, is that the good and caring people don't know this about themselves, individually.

And when I use the phrase, *know this about themselves, individually*, I am referring to knowing on an emotional and spiritual level where acceptance takes place. I am not referring to the intellectual level where belief takes place. The strings and props of being nice are holding us up, giving the illusion that we are actually free to be *who* we are, which is fundamentally good. But, when either internal or external conflict abounds, then violence, cruelty,

Who We Are

condemnation, and self-righteous indignation become the preferred behavior. The strings and props of being nice are instantly discarded in favor of revealing what is truly at large in our society: an essence and basic nature that is *something other than good, bad,* or *evil.*

For this reason, the American way of life, historically and presently, can parallel an existence that is self-restricting and imprisoning. Inside the cage of domination, which our way of life is based upon, exist increased violence, cruelty, condemnation, and self-righteous indignation. Individually and collectively, we simply are not free inside this cage to be *who* we are innately. "But, if you open the cage, it's happy." Why? For two basic reasons: the fundamental good an individual embodies and the qualities that comprise *who* that individual is innately is valued both by the individual and his or her community.

Conversely, the American way of life can also be self-restricting and imprisoning because it places a greater value on *what* an individual is rather than on *who* an individual is inherently. In addition, recognition of an individual is primarily based on power. And power is derived as a result of appearance, position, and prestige. The self-restricting and imprisoning condition occurs as a result of

What We Are

the personal sacrifice an individual will make in order to adapt and adjust to this *what* scheme. And the personal sacrifice is usually a surrendering of the pristine qualities that comprise *who* an individual is intrinsically.

But, let us not forget that an individual who knows that his or her essence is undeniably good would not choose to surrender *who* he or she is so as to fit into a *what* way of life. There is a close relationship between not knowing *who* one is intrinsically and not knowing that one's essence is basically good with surrendering one's self to a *what* way of life. A significant problem that this way of life can create for an individual is *what* he or she is usually plays to an audience devoid of *who* that individual is innately. The inability to bring forth an essence that is fundamentally good can produce intense moments of personal loneliness.

An argument can justifiably be made that for many Americans, life within this cage, generally speaking, is excellent. There are a substantial number of Americans who are treated and fed better than at any other time during our young history. And the argument can also justifiably be made that we do give ourselves everything we seem to want, even when we cannot afford the expense. This expense is one that is often of a financial, physical, emotional, and spiritual nature.

Popular phrases that justify the expense are, "I owe it to myself," "I deserve this," and "I've worked hard." Individually and collectively, we never seem to forget for one moment that this is a land of opportunity and surplus. We take a righteous position that warrants our taking from others as well as from this land, rather than simply giving for the sake of enhancement. Unfortunately, opportunity and surplus oftentimes is at the expense of the dignity, respect, and integrity of either another individual, this land that we temporarily occupy, or one's self.

Robert Johnson, author of the book *Inner Work*, states: "In modern society, we have reached the point at which we try to get by without acknowledging the inner life at all. We act as though there were no unconscious, no realm of the soul, as though we could live full lives by fixating ourselves completely on the external material world. We try to deal with all the issues of life by external means: making more money, starting a love affair, or accomplishing something in the material world. But we discover to our surprise that the inner world is a reality that we ultimately have to face. If we try to ignore the inner

What We Are

world, as most of us do, the unconscious will find its way into our lives through pathology, our psychosomatic systems, compulsions, depressions, and neuroses."

Still, we remain locked inside a way of life that is self-restricting and imprisoning because, individually and collectively, we are persona-and performance-driven. A painful admission of this is the emptiness and barrenness that is often spoken of by courageous individuals who have fallen under the wheel of this fast-paced way of life. Courageous, because they are no longer willing to protect a way of life that holds little value for the dignity, respect, and emotional integrity of an individual. After investing a substantial amount of one's life in a frantic pursuit of goals that simply pertain to *what* an individual is, the results do not justify the personal sacrifice. To be cast aside due to age, fading beauty, a soft body, or a better lover is a heart-breaking reality to accept. Anguish and disappointment do not describe in an adequate fashion the depth of the pain that accompanies this heartbreak.

During the developmental and adolescent stages, an individual basically is not educated, supported, nor encouraged to live a life based on *who* he or she is intrinsically. So, it is not too long after settling into late adolescence and young adulthood that an internal ache and discomfort is felt. And that internal ache is the longing and yearning to reconnect with what is authentic and natural within one's self. The personal sacrifice of an individual's authentic and natural self is inclined to occur because of the emergence of a powerful and seductive illusion. In the *what you are* world, it is easy to tempt an individual with recognition and power, especially when there has been a yearning and longing for these experiences since birth. It is difficult to deny the seductiveness of the illusion when there has been an absence of suitable emotional and spiritual grounding during the early stages of an individual's life.

From yet another book authored by Robert Johnson, *Owning Your Own Shadow*, he states: "We all are born whole but somehow the culture demands that we live out only part of our nature and refuse other parts of our inheritance. We divide the self into an ego and a shadow because our culture insists that we behave in a particular manner. This is our legacy from having eaten of the fruit of the tree of knowledge in the Garden of Eden. Culture takes away the simple human in us, but gives us more complex and sophisticated power. One can make a forceful argument that children should not be subjected to this division too soon or they will be robbed of childhood;

they should be allowed to remain in the Garden of Eden until they are strong enough to stand the cultural process without being broken by it."

A way of life that temporarily honors *what* you are will fail to live up to its promise to quench that internal thirst. *What* you are simply cannot satisfy the inner thirst to experience *who* you are innately. As a result of this societal failure to mandate and properly educate an individual to an essence and basic nature that is good, the door to the cage is locked. It is locked by what governs our way of life. And what governs our way of life is what governs relationships, both with self and other people. The cage, individually and collectively, is locked by the practice of domination. But this same door can be unlocked, individually and collectively, by using a model of cooperation that honors and respects the intrinsic good that an individual embodies.

Inside this cage of domination, where emotional and spiritual freedom is restricted, an individual is taught at an early age the benefits of being nice. Regretfully so, being nice offers a social cover for the absence of knowing that an individual is basically good. Belief must replace knowledge if the practice of domination is to be effective.

Who We Are

An individual is simply taught to look and act *as if* he or she is good, rather than to live from the vantage point that one's essence and basic nature *is* undeniably good. Oftentimes, an individual will state in a matter-of-fact tone, "I know that I am a good person." However, when this same individual is faced with either internal or external conflict, he or she will resort to violent behavior, cruelty, condemnation, or harsh judgement. As a means of contending with conflict, this humiliating and demeaning behavior is directed at another individual or one's self.

Again, internal or external conflict will be the experience that separates the individual who *believes* that his or her essence and basic nature is good from the individual who *knows* this particular truth about self. A person will use harsh judgement, condemnation, cruelty, or violence as a means to cope with his or her conflict, if being nice is a way of life. If a person knows that his or her essence is undeniably good, then conflict will be experienced in its fullness, but not at the personal expense of another or self.

Frankly, being nice is at a price. The price is the sacrifice of one's undeniable good essence and basic nature, which represents the authentic self. The sacrifice of one's authentic self is made as a result of not being

What We Are

educated and supported as to the inherent qualities that comprise the good that an individual embodies. Therefore, *who* an individual is with respect to innate qualities is disaffirmed, and the pursuit to develop a *what* persona takes precedence. We are taught how necessary it is to be nice, which is set aside when either internal or external conflict occurs. It is deemed appropriate to resort to behavior that exemplifies an essence that is *something other than good* or *bad* when there is conflict.

One consolation is the inappropriateness of using evil behavior as a means of recourse when reacting to either internal or external conflict. The criminal justice system and mental institutions have been established to counter this type of reaction to conflict. However, within our society it is appropriate to morally assassinate an individual, but not to physically assassinate. It is appropriate to morally steal from another individual, but we cannot physically steal. If the reader is in doubt of these claims, then I would suggest reviewing our history as a society with respect to women, Native, African, and Hispanic Americans, gays and lesbians, and Jewish Americans.

The door to the cage, both individually and collectively, will open—and open on a permanent basis—when the truth about one's self is finally accepted. Individually, the compulsive need to seek from another what he or she already possesses, that is, an essence and basic nature that is undeniably good, will cease. Collectively, the need to perpetuate debasing behavior towards a group of people because of the color of their skin, sexual preference, choice of religion, or gender orientation will cease as well. When the innate qualities of compassion, genius, community, autonomy, authority, passion, and emotional integrity are recognized as good, then the door to the cage will open.

From the beginning of Western civilization, what officially sanctioned the practice of domination was Orthodox Christianity. Young America made no exception to this custom in the beginning of its existence. Its new immigrants carried over with them the same caste system and aristocratic way of life that they were frantically fleeing. It was extremely difficult for the Indian and slave to argue against the injustices being perpetuated against them, once the early European had arrived upon the shores of America. It was difficult indeed, for the early European came armed with his advanced weaponry and his Bible.

What has sanctioned the practice of domination by Orthodox Christianity is the implementation of the doctrine that is said to establish the fact that an individual's essence and basic nature is inherently corrupt. Biblical scripture, in particular the second and third chapters of Genesis, have been designated as a primary source that substantiates man and woman's corruptness. I might add that Biblical scripture also submits that woman's essence and basic nature is more corrupt than man's. This particular distinction carries with it a responsibility by her to suppress this essence and basic nature, except, of course, when it is to man's advantage to experience her sensuality.

In her book, *A God Who Looks Like Me*, Patricia Lynn Reilly informs the reader: "Although Original Sin is a shaming idea for all children, male and female, it carries an extra stigma for the girl-child, since we were taught that it was definitely Eve and not Adam who took the first bite of the forbidden apple. Eve shows up again and again in women's writings. She reminds us that we are responsible for humankind's sin. The early church fathers would be proud of us. We learned their lessons well."

In 1 Peter 3: 3-5, he warns women: "Do not adorn yourselves outwardly by braiding your hair, and by wearing gold ornaments or fine clothing; rather, let your adornment be the inner self with the lasting beauty of a gentle and quiet spirit, which is very precious in God's sight. It was in this way long ago that the holy women who hoped in God used to adorn themselves by committing themselves to their husbands." I continue to find it puzzling that man will decree to woman how she needs to present herself to him and to God, yet will vehemently reject the notion that he is practicing domination. Deriving conviction from doctrine produced and decreed sacred during an era when women were horribly oppressed, man still maintains an inflexible and domineering stance with respect to how women should conduct themselves.

There are a host of religions in our society that are not recognized by Orthodox Christianity as being legitimate Christian religions. The reason behind the rejection is because they do not accept basic Orthodox Christian doctrine. For example, certain religions, like Christian Science do not accept the doctrine of Original Sin as the basis for creation. And there are other religions in American society that simply will not accept Paul and Peter's negative attitudes towards women. Christian Science, Unity, and Unitarian would fall into this category.

These and other religions that are not accepted by Orthodox Christianity establish a difference between the inspired writings and uninspired writings of the Bible.

What We Are

Where woman is made responsible for the downfall of humankind and where she is mandated by man to serve man and God in a specific manner, this would consist of uninspired writings. Where the word of Christ Jesus is spoken or the dignity of an individual is preserved, this would comprise inspired writings of the Bible.

However, these supposedly non-Christian religions share with Orthodox Christianity the practice of domination. The most obvious examples are the directives that each will persistently convey to its faithful as well as to the inquisitive. One persistent directive is how the way to personal salvation is through that particular religion or spiritual pathway's doors. Each religion or spiritual path is promoted as being better than or more effective than the others. In addition, there is often a veiled directive that is gently, but tenaciously offered, to those entering the doors for the first time. That is, if a person is to take advantage of the principles either taught or preached, then he or she would accomplish this best by learning and speaking the language.

But more importantly, the practice of domination is exhibited by these religions, spiritual paths, and Orthodox Christianity by insisting that personal legitimacy, redemption, and salvation be pursued through external sources.

Who We Are

And that external source is usually their specific path, and with their hierarchy acting as the medium between the individual and God. Not all religions or spiritual paths openly teach or preach that one's essence is *something other than good, bad*, or *evil*. Nonetheless, most seem to advance that theory, since the individual is not capable of achieving this one-on-one experience with their God or higher being through their own efforts.

I realize that I have made sweeping generalizations about those religions and spiritual paths rejected by Orthodox Christianity as being legitimate Christian religions. I understand that there are a number of religions and spiritual paths that do not want to be associated with Christianity, and are pleased to have no affiliation. To those religions and spiritual paths that I may have offended with my generalizations, I apologize. It is not my intent to be offensive, but to point out my personal observations. To those religions and spiritual paths that do desire to be associated with Christianity but are still rejected as being legitimate Christian religions, I apologize if I have overstated my observations.

My personal experiences with religions and spiritual paths both inside and outside of Orthodox Christianity have

What We Are

been creditable. However, I confess that what I have learned from being raised in the Orthodox Christian and non-Orthodox Christian religions does not give me a license to know what goes on inside the walls of all churches or spiritual paths. I also confess that what I have learned from having visited with a number of churches and spiritual paths and having studied numerous religions does not give me a license to know all. Again, I am speaking from my personal experiences, which I know are limited.

Nevertheless, I do believe that Orthodox Christianity and other forms of religion or spiritual paths must take into account a significant aspect of an individual's development. If they are to be effective in today's society, then the manner in which a person is raised cannot be ignored and treated as irrelevant. Not unless, of course, the objective of the religion or spiritual path is to practice domination. It is not what transpired before one's birth that renders an individual's essence as *something other than good, bad, or evil.*

Orthodox Christianity insists that we, on an individual basis, accept the doctrine that a person's basic nature is corrupt. I stand in direct opposition to this teaching. It is what happens after an individual's birth that teaches him or her to accept and embrace this negative self-perception. There are religions and spiritual paths that insist on putting a new coat of shellac on a floor that is worn with emotional and spiritual wounds. No religion or spiritual path can inform and urge an individual to believe that he or she is good and have that belief remain anchored. And we know that the belief that one is good is lost when internal or external conflict occurs.

Children and adolescents are raised in our American culture to neglect and abandon the truth that one's essence is undeniably good. This is accomplished by culturally insisting that *what* a person is externally carries a greater value and significance than *who* that person is internally. The intrinsic value of the innate qualities that comprise *who* an individual is simply is set aside as insignificant. In its place, great effort is exerted to develop a persona that is performance-, position-, and prestige-oriented. *What* an individual is simply is not an answer for an essence that is *something other than good, bad,* or *evil.* We reject and denounce one another, including self, on the grounds of *who* we are because little value is given to this aspect of one's self.

Violence, cruelty, condemnation, and harsh judgement are produced by individuals who believe that their

What We Are

essence and basic nature is *something other than good, bad,* or *evil.* Murder and hate crimes are committed by individuals who accept that their essence is *evil.* Insanity is the result of the same belief about one's self. Alcoholism, drug addiction, bulimia, anorexia, compulsive gambling, and theft are the results of an individual who accepts that his or her essence is *bad.* Slander and gossip are behaviors that emanate from an individual who believes that his or her essence is *something other than good.*

I stand deeply saddened by what is transpiring within our country today. Hate crimes and crimes of indiscriminate violence are being directed at specified ethnic groups, adolescents, little children, and the elderly, not to mention the continued assaults against women. These crimes are occurring at an alarming rate, and we seem horribly dominated by this behavior. Individuals who believe and accept that their essence and basic nature is *evil* are finding deplorable ways to impact our daily lives with violence and cruelty. From January 14, 1999 to August 10, 1999, at least eleven multiple shootings have taken place throughout our country. The question still remains on the table for this society to answer. When are we, as a society, going to have the courage to face this problem of increased violence, cruelty, and condemnation with a sense of honesty and urgency?

Who We Are

The core issue that is propelling this increase in violent behavior, which includes cruelty, harsh judgement, and condemnation is not gun control, more security measures and prayer in our schools, or stiffer day-trading standards. The core issue is how the practice of domination is being carried out by individuals who accept that their essence and basic nature is either *bad* or *evil*. Because the practice of domination is an appropriate way of life in our society, these individuals seek to manifest the severity of their illnesses through this practice.

They are feeling dominated by either their mental disorder or mental illnesses and the natural reaction is to then dominate others. We can begin addressing this national crisis by making a concerted effort to educate and teach our children, adolescents, and young adults that the very essence and basic nature that they embody is undeniably good. We can address this problem by supporting and encouraging one other to live a life that is based on the inherent qualities that comprise that basic good, which actually is *who* we are innately.

However, my outrage at what is occurring within our country does not stop at addressing the increase in violent behavior. My outrage extends to the media, educators,

What We Are

public officials, and parents who accept and give credibility to the violence and cruelty that is occurring within our schools. I was absolutely horrified to watch on the evening news on August 10, 1999, the town of Williams Bay, Wisconsin engaged in a simulated shooting drill, which took place at one of its public schools. A few of the male students were completely dressed in camouflage outfits brandishing high-powered rifles with blanks, shooting at their principal and fellow students. These would-be villains were forcing their fellow students to run for their lives as well as detaining some and holding them as hostages.

SWAT teams participated in the simulated drill, along with local police and fire department personnel. Parents stood passively in a nearby parking lot watching their children run for their lives with fake blood dripping down their clothes. Parents watched as children carried or dragged "wounded" classmates across the campus to areas of safety. The school superintendent, Peter Geissel, justified conducting this grotesque operation with a statement that questions his ability to separate from this type of emotional and psychological domination. He stated, "Administrators have felt a real responsibility to worry about kids' safety. It used to be bus safety and playground safety and those kinds of things. So this is a new facet that none of us enjoy, but we need to do it."

It is perfectly appropriate for school administrators, teachers, city officials, and students to gather together and construct various strategies to counter disasters and tragedies of any nature. But, you do not, and I reiterate, do not, involve the children to the degree that these children were involved during this shooting drill. Having male students dressed in camouflage outfits brandishing high-powered rifles with blanks, shooting at their principal and fellow students is absolutely absurd. Having students running for their lives with fake blood on their clothing is appalling. And having children dragging one another to areas of safety while in anticipation of losing their lives is beyond the ridiculous. Even though this was a simulated drill, why traumatize children before the trauma? Why introduce to these children the mentality of victimization before they have had an opportunity to embrace for themselves a way of life that is based on an undeniable individual good?

As an African American male, I know all too well the experiences of being a victim of racism and classism in my own country. I have emotionally and psychologically survived these horrible experiences because I refuse to

What We Are

be victimized by them. I understand that the white supremacist, the bigot, and the racist have established a mindset of superiority that is historically based on *what* he or she is, and that is simply being white. This particular individual has learned to accept that his or her essence and basic nature is either *bad* or *evil,* simply because there is a lack of knowledge to the contrary. The inherent good and those qualities that comprise this basic good were never mirrored back to this individual. Hence, *who* this individual is innately cannot be made manifest in his or her life. As a result, the practice of domination replaces a practice of cooperation as a way of life.

Women who are subjected to sexism, Native, Hispanic, and Asian Americans who are subjected to racism, Jewish Americans who are subjected to religious persecution, gay and lesbian Americans who are subjected to homophobia must resist the temptation to be victimized by these injustices as well. To resist being victimized by demeaning and debasing behavior means to efficiently disallow the internalization that one's essence and basic nature is *something other than good, bad,* or *evil.* We may indeed experience being the victim of another individual's injustice. However, it is the individual's responsibility who

Who We Are

has suffered that injustice not to absorb the notion that his or her essence and basic nature is less than good.

The news reporter, Jim Avila, who covered this unfortunate event for "NBC Nightly News," ended his story by stating, "Because too often in America, even in one of its safest small towns, people here say, the classroom is no place for innocence anymore." My anger hit decibels that were not readable nor understandable. I think it is extremely sad that there are individuals in our country who are ready and willing to surrender the classroom to those individuals who believe and accept that their essence and basic nature is *bad* or *evil*. The classroom is a place for innocence, and our children ought to enjoy the right of expecting to have this experience preserved.

Under no circumstances should we, as a society, institutionalize this form of emotional, psychological, and physical domination. Under no circumstances should we, as a society, give credibility to this increase in violence and cruelty that is so desperately wanting to hold our country in its grasp. We have a national and international policy in place that states we will never negotiate with a terrorist. Why should we then negotiate or reduce our way of life to accommodate that individual or individuals who desire to dominate with his or her mental disorder or mental illness?

We, individually and collectively, simply cannot continue adapting and adjusting to the problems that are created by the practice of domination. We are faced with the challenge to change our internal beliefs about ourselves individually and about one another, as a society. The truth that still awaits our individual and collective embrace and acceptance is the basic good that each and every person embodies and the honor that is due each and every person for *who* he or she is, innately.

Who We Are

"Self-forgiveness brings forth that beautiful spirit of understanding and nurturing that allows an individual to access his or her dignity and grace, and to reach out to that sweet spirit that resides in others."

Bradley Lee Ulrich

What We Are

"In order to stand together with others in a true sense of community, an individual must first be willing to stand alone in the community of one.

When an individual is willing to embrace his or her sense of aloneness or loneliness, the personal treasures therein are revealed to that individual. The myth of internal poverty and barrenness oftentimes associated with feeling lonely and alone is transformed into the reality of personal sovereignty, self-respect, and courage. At this point, an individual can truly stand in reverence of one's own and another's individuality."

Bradley Lee Ulrich

WORKS CITED

1. **Steven J. Russell**, *BEING NICE AT A PRICE: Emotional Domination, Depression, and the Search For Autonomy*, Publisher, Puget Sound Press, 6523 California Ave., SW #292, Seattle, WA. 98136.

2. **Jean Shinoda Bolen, M.D.**, *Ring of Power: The Abandoned Child, The Authoritarian Father, and The Disempowered Feminine*, Publisher, HarperCollins Publishers, 10 East 53rd Street, New York, NY 10022.

3. **Clayborne Carson, Ph.D.**, *The Autobiography of Martin Luther King, Jr.,* Publisher, Time Warner AudioBooks, A division of Time Warner Trade Publishing, 1271 Avenue of the Americas, New York, NY 10020.

What We Are

4. **Robert A. Johnson**, *Inner Work*, Publisher, HarperCollins Publishers, 10 East 53rd Street, New York, NY 10022.

5. **Robert A. Johnson**, *Owning Your Own Shadow*, Publisher, HarperCollins Publishers, 10 East 53rd Street, New York, NY 10022.

6. **Patricia Lynn Reilly**, *A God Who Looks Like Me*, Publisher, Ballantine Books, A division of Random House, Inc., New York, NY 10022.

INDEX

1 Peter 3: 3-5 156.
1960s 129.
1971 130.
1999 baseball season 60.
301st and 302nd 130.

A man who loved his family 87.
A place for innocence 167.
A way of life 29,39.
Able to love 94.
Absolute good 32,132.
Absolutely horrified 164.
Abstract freedom versus real freedom 5.
Academic credentials 41.
Academic probation 102.
Academic pursuits 64.
Accepting the truth 16.
Accountability 58,64,66,69, 81,105,109,114,115, 120,127.
Accountable 13.
Accountant and auditor 8.
Act as if 153.
Acting good 13.
Acts of indignity 119.
Adapt and adjust 15,39,148.
Adult absurdity 45.
Adult caretakers 97.
Adult sports enthusiast 31.
Adversarial in nature 31.
Adversarial position 50.
Adversary 17.
Affirmative Action 36,113.
Afford the expense 148.
African 20.
African Americans 80,99,106, 111,112,137.
Airplane pilot 56.
Alcohol and drug counselor 8,9, 11,16.
Alcoholism and drug addiction 9,87,133.
All corners of the world 141.
All-male high school 100.
American culture 44.
American society 20,27.
American way of life 81,144.
An artist 88.
An essence and basic nature 135.
Anguish and disappointment 150.
Anorexia 162.
Antagonistic 50.
Article for publication 124.
Asian Americans 20,166.
Assaults against women 162.
Assistant principal 101,102.
Assuredly good 116.
Atonement is redemption. 121.
August 10, 1999 164.
Authentic and natural 151.

What We Are

Authentic self 153.
Autonomy 4,15,47,72.
Avila, Jim 167.

Bad or evil 99.
Bad person 9,14.
Baptist minister 105.
Baseball fan 61.
Baseball pitcher 56.
Basic good 168.
Basic nature is corrupt 160.
Basic rights and freedoms 79.
Basic survival 143.
Basically good 74,146,152, 168 .
Basketball and football 105.
Basketball scholarship 92.
Bathed in good 105.
"because I am your mother." 93.
Being nice 13,63,146,152, 153.
Believes 153.
Below fifty-percent 89.
Belt or tree limb 92.
Benefits of writing 127,128.
Best and brightest 41.
Betrayal 49.
"black listed," 100.
Black man living in America 129, 133.
Blackouts and drunkenness 8.
Blame 29.
Blind eye and a deaf ear 135.
Bolen, Jean Shinoda M.D. 38.

Brandishing high-powered rifles 164,165.
Brown, Kevin 33,60.
Bulimia 162.
Bureaucratic agencies 60.
Burton, LeVar 98.
Businesswoman 82.
"But, if you open the cage, it's happy." 140,147.

Cage of domination 147,152.
California, San Jose 129.
Camaraderie 60.
Camouflage outfits 164.
Carson, Clayborne 98.
Caste system 155.
Causes are irrelevant 136.
Champion 142.
Character 31.
Chemotherapy 95.
Chicago 83,94,100,129.
Chicago's West Side 8.
Child-rearing practice 49.
Children 28,29,30,33,43,47,58, 68,73,97,161.
Christ Jesus 158.
Christian churches 43.
Christian ideology 45.
Christian religions 157.
Christian Science 157.
Christianity 80.
Civil rights leader 105.
Civil rights movement 106,107, 116.
Civilized behavior 69.
Class, gender, and race 126.

Who We Are

Cleansing experience 121.
Clinton, Hillary 52.
Clinton, President 43,52.
Club of toughness 103.
Cohesive community 67.
Cohesiveness of family 79.
Collective focus 30,44.
Color of their skin, 155.
Columbine High School 26.
Commitment and conviction 98.
Common humanity 142.
Community-minded 86.
Compassion 19,46,98,116.
Compassion and redemption 120.
Compassion for one's suffering 121.
Compassionate 51.
Competitiveness 31.
Complex and sophisticated 151.
Compliance 48.
Concern for people 12.
Condemnation 85.
Conflict 3,15,17,18,28,36,39, 43, 46,50,53,58,68,70, 80,93,117,153,161.
Congeniality 28.
Contemporary trademark 112.
Contemptuous behavior 2,106.
Conviction 40,56.
Conviction and courage 120.
Copperfield, David 146.
Core issue 45.
Counseling or therapy 55.

Coup d'état 2.
Courageous 150.
Cowardly 102.
Crashed and burned 14.
Creative process 88.
Creativity 11.
Credibility 66.
Credibility to emotions 114.
Criminal charges 101.
Criminal justice system 154.
Crisp fall afternoon 129.
Criticism 35.
Cruelty 127.
Cruelty, and violence 16, 22,29.

Dangerous weapon 29.
Day-Lewis, Cecil 126.
Deathly feared 103.
Debasing behavior 118.
Debate symptoms 39.
Decision-making 34.
Declarations of forgiveness 121.
Decrease violence 145.
Dedicated mail carrier 87.
Deep financial pockets 33.
Deeply felt intimacy 94.
Deeply hurt 132.
Degrading judgement 117.
Degree of coherency 79.
Degree of sincerity 106.
Demean and debase 142.
Democratic party 36.
Depression 71.
Destiny as a leader 75.
Destroyed the manuscript 133.

What We Are

Dignity 3,40,53,56,63,80.
Dignity and integrity
   117,144,145.
Disallow the internalization
   166.
Disapproval 131.
Disobedience 87.
Dominant culture 113.
Dominate 17,19.
Domination versus
   cooperation 5.
Donaldson, Sam 43.
"Don't mess with Eric, 103.
Door to the cage 154.
Downfall of humankind 158.
Dr. King's eulogy
   and burial 107.
Dreadful Friday 134.
Drunken stupor 132.
"dummy," 88.

Early European 155.
Economic agenda. 59.
Economic domination 34, 60.
Ego 48.
Ego and a shadow 151.
Elgin State Hospital 91.
Emasculating 91.
Emasculation 103.
Embodiment of good 1,11,14,
   21,40,54.
Embodiment of humility. 67.
Embody this lie 134.
Emotional abuse 87.
Emotional and spiritual
   deficiency 134.

Emotional and spiritual skills
   22.
Emotional despair 5.
Emotional domination 29.
Emotional integrity 28,33,47,54,
   66,67,69,109,116,125,150.
Emotional mirrors 30.
Emotional, physical, and
   spiritual relief 17.
Emotional pleas 101.
Emotionally murdered 54.
Emotionally recover 95.
Emphatic lie 16.
Emphatic no 132.
Employer 58,64.
Empowerment 38.
Emptiness and barrenness 150.
Enigma 54.
Errors in judgement 46.
Escalation of dominance 44.
Essence and basic nature 9,11,
   13,18,39,44,47,49,51,53,
   65,70,113,118,120,122,
   134,136,144,152,155,162.
Essence is good 117,124,125,
   148.
Essence not being good 108.
Essence of good 84.
Essence or basic nature 62, 68,
   97,109,110.
Essence that is good. 128.
Essential good 143.
Establishing credibility 127.
Eternal little boy 94.
Ethnicity 106.
European 20.

Who We Are

European American male 81.
Evil and bad self-perceptions 87.
Evil behavior 154.
Evil person 14.
Exercise in futility 118.
Experience her sensuality 156.
Experts 40.
Extend one's self 123.
External conflict 3.
External validation 41.

Façade 85.
Fading beauty 150.
Failed relationships 14.
Fake blood 164.
Family legacy 136.
Family of origin 52.
Family vehicle 34.
Far too destructive 27.
Father 87,88,89,131,134.
Father passed away 132.
Fear and distrust 143.
"feel a sense of somebodyness." 99.
Feel good 16.
Feeling of embarrassment 81.
Feelings of fear 84.
Fell in love 97.
Fellow students 130.
Fight the cancer 96.
Financial responsibilities 92.
Fistfight 100,103.
Forbidden apple 156.
Forgiveness 98.
Forlorn and downhearted 91.
Formidable good 20.
Forte of our young people 68.
Free enterprise system 141.
Friend or foe 75.
Fulfil this role 12.
Fundamental good 86, 95,147.
Fundamentally solid and good 79.
Fundamentally sound and good. 107.

Garden of Eden 151.
Gays and lesbians 154.
Geissel, Peter 164.
Gender orientation 155.
Genesis 156.
Genius 20.
Giving to another 124.
Good 3,97.
Good and caring people 146.
Good person 11,48,54,82,133.
Good versus nice 5.
Government regulation 141.
Grade school 88.
Grandmother 90.
Grandparents 136.
Great remorse and sorrow 132.
Great-grandparents 20.
Greed 67.
Grodin, Charles 42.
Guardian 40,47,63,144.
Guardian of one another's dignity 30,142.
Gun control 163.
Guns 43,44,45.

What We Are

Harsh and brutal punishment 87.
Healing agents 122.
Heart attack 96.
Heart break 132.
Heart-breaking 49.
Heartfelt compassion 67.
"Hello, this is the twenty-first 143.
Helping profession 14.
High school 88.
High school graduation 132.
High school teacher 56.
High-ticket prices 61.
Hispanic 20.
Hispanic Americans 154.
Historically and presently 147.
History books 80.
Hit decibels 167.
Homophobia 27,166.
Honesty and urgency? 162.
Horrible experiences 165.
Hostages 135,164.
Howard-Leonard, Jane Alpha 98.
Human spirit 75.
Humiliation 38,117.
Humility 32,69,122.
Hurtful behavior 2.

"**I** am simply writing about my 131.
"I deserve this," 149.
"I know that I am a good person." 153.
"I never thought that you would make it." 104.
"I never thought you would make it." 89.
"I owe it to myself," 149.
"I want to look good so that I feel good" 5.
Imperfection 67.
Implied consent 120.
Importance of writing 113.
Impressionable athlete 31.
"In order to win, 31.
In-depth personal examination 124.
Inability of people 143.
Inability to forgive 52.
Inadequate, and not enough 18.
Incapable of loving 134.
Incessant need 56.
Income and taxes 8.
Increased violence 43,143.
Increasing revenues 60.
Indian and slave 155.
Indifference to human life 73.
Indignity 19,114,115,119.
Individual and collective responsibility 144.
Individual and God 159.
Individual redemption 110.
Individual's development 160.
Inflexible and domineering 157.
Infrastructure 63.
Inherent authority 46,128.
Inherent good 22,40,166.
Inherently corrupt 156.

Who We Are

Inherently sound and good 128, 136.
Innate characteristics 32.
Innate good 19,20,32.
Innate worth 38.
Innately good 16.
Innately possesses 125.
Inner acceptance 39.
Inner belief 10.
Inner garment 122.
Inner vacuum 135.
Inspired writings 157.
Institution of sports. 56.
Integrity 21,30,42.
Internal ache 151.
Internal antagonism 52.
Internal disturbance 84.
Internal lie 53.
Internal thirst 152.
Internalized beliefs 15.
Internalized self-hatred 133.
Internalized weakness 45.
Intrinsic good 152.
Intrinsic value 72,99,145.
Introspective 115.
Intuitive 11.
Irrevocably good 122,137.
Issue of essence 138.
Issues of domination 111.
Italian American 82.
"I've worked hard." 149.

Jamestown College 89,92, 128.
January 14, 1999 162.
Jewish Americans 154.

Johnson, Davey 32.
Johnson, Robert 149,151.
Journal recording 121.
Judeo/Christian 80.
Justifiable anger 62.

Kindness and generosity 94.
King, Dr. Martin Luther Jr. 98,116.
King, Larry 42.
Know that we, individually, are good 23.
Know this about themselves 146.
Knows 153.
Kristol, Bill 43.

Lack of concern 88.
Lack of depth 15.
Lacking self-confidence 86.
Ladder of despair 134.
Larger-than-life reputation 12.
Legal domination 36.
Legitimacy 40.
Legitimate 84.
Legitimate place 13.
Leonard, Lorenzo Robert 98.
Less than good 17,23,46,54.
Liberalism and skepticism 106.
Life within this cage 148.
Life-enhancing 125.
Literally vaporized 112.
Little boy 11.
Local bakery 104.
Local car wash 96.
Local press 129.

What We Are

Local television. 61.
Long-standing friends 17.
Look at one's self 114.
Look outside 73.
Loss of not feeling loved 94.
Lost virtue 64.
Loved ones 14.
Lucrative contract 61.

Machine shop class 100.
Macho and fearless. 104.
Making more money 149.
Malcolm X 105.
Male students 165.
Male-dominated 83.
Mandated by man 158.
Manuscript unacceptable 134.
Marital differences 91.
Marketing strategies 129.
Marriage 34.
Masculinity 104.
Material wealth 20.
Matthews, Chris 42.
Men and women 137.
Mental anguish 5.
Mental disorder 163.
Mentality of victimization 165.
Methods of resolution 27.
Meticulous staffing notes 11.
Mid- to late forties 55.
Mid-1980s 41.
Miniature adults 28.
Mirrored back 166.
Mirrors and echoes 49.
"misery loves company," 120.

Model of cooperation 27,30, 31, 38, 42,66, 74,75,78, 105, 106,145,152.
Model of domination 27,31,38,57,69,72,74,75, 78,145.
Model of weakness 28.
Moral crisis 79.
Moral fiber 69.
Moral issues 52.
Morally assassinate 154.
Morally legitimate 19.
More corrupt than man's 156.
Morning ritual 58.
Mother 90,91,95,130,134.
Mother and son 96.
Motorists 29.
Mounting carnage 30.
Multiple shootings 162.
Murder and hate 162.
Mutuality 57.
My intent 13.

Naïve and unrealistic 143.
Nation of diverse cultures 74.
Native 20.
Native Americans 80.
Natural flow of feelings 34.
Natural resources 74.
Natural to feel hurt and angry 135.
Negative self-perception 114.
Neighborhood bully 103.
New coat of shellac 161.
New way of living 125.
Nice 51.

Who We Are

Nice behavior 48,50.
Nice person 48,50,53,59, 83,93.
Nobility and integrity 143.
Nobility of character 69,142.
Non-Christian religions 158.
Non-Orthodox Christian 160.
Not enough 2.
Not equal to 93,99,105.
Not good enough 71.
Number of churches 160.

Obedient 65.
Often cried 95.
Omething other than good, bad, or evil. 147.
"One day Mom" 96.
One-on-one experience 159.
Opportunity and surplus. 149.
Oregon, Portland 11,94,95.
Original Sin 156,157.
Orthodox Christianity 155,157,159,160.
Our ancestors 21.
Our schools 27.
Outrage 163.
Oval Office. 53.
Over three hundred people 134.
Over-stimulation 68.
Ownership of feelings 114.

Pageantry 4.
Pain and money 13.
Pain-filled relationships 55.

Painful challenge 1.
Painful process 126.
Painting or sculpting 88.
Paper routes 92.
Parents 20,87,97,102,129,164.
"Parity is not the American way" 33.
Passion 66,155.
Performance 55.
Performance oriented 48.
Performance-driven 150.
Period of enlightenment 106.
Perpetuating the lie 108.
Personal accountability 27.
Personal affront 115,117.
Personal agendas 29.
Personal and interpersonal conflicts 41.
Personal and interpersonal problems 40,45.
Personal authority 65,84.
Personal autonomy 115.
Personal commitment 5.
Personal confrontation 107.
Personal dignity 78.
Personal discipline 126.
Personal freedom 140,144.
Personal frustration 64.
Personal ideology 144.
Personal lawsuit 102.
Personal legitimacy 69,128,158.
Personal living hell 10.
Personal loneliness 148.
Personal observations 159.
Personal responsibility 2.
Personal sacrifice 150.

181

What We Are

Personal scope 123.
Personal vendetta 90.
Personal work 46.
Philosophical disagreement 105.
Physical confrontations 102.
Physical domination 35,167.
Physically assassinate 154.
Pinnacle and clarity 123.
Pinnacle of one's intelligence 124.
Place of depravation. 116.
Place of employment 57.
Plastic surgery 101.
Police station 101.
Political affiliation 142.
Political and economic agendas 41.
Political domination 36.
Political right, left, or middle 141,145.
Positive and supportive 130.
Possessed integrity 105.
Power and control 138.
Power and dominance 37.
Power and influence 104.
Powerful denial system 10.
Practical solutions 42.
Practice of accountability 65.
Practice of cooperation 22,166.
Practice of domination 19,22, 27,30,31,33,34,36,38,39, 43,55,58,59,61,63,70, 79,118,122,123,125, 126,135,137,152,155, 158,163,166,168.

Practice of integrity 64.
Prayer back into the schools 43.
Prayer in our schools 163.
Preparation for work 59.
Prestige-oriented 161.
Preying on the weak 63.
Primarily based on power 147.
Primary relationships 57, 81, 91,110.
Private practice. 16.
Privilege and entitlement 32.
Process of writing 113,126.
Profit orientated 59.
Promoting the truth 108.
Properly educate 152.
Prose and poetry 131.
Proven wrong 131.
Psychological domination 35.
Psychology of our society 106.
Public demeanor 45.
Public schools 43.

Quality of good 56.
Quality of relationships 113.

Racial and social equality 110.
Racial attitudes and practices 107.
Racial tension and polarity 107.
Racially insulting words 102.
Racism 99.
Racism and sexism 117.
Racist and sexist joke 61.
Reactionary behavior 37.
Real responsibility 164.
Recipient of contempt 63.

Who We Are

Redeeming 10.
Redemption 113,121,159.
Reilly, Patricia Lynn 156.
Reject and denounce 161.
Relationships 17,18.
Relationships with women 94.
Religions and spiritual paths 160.
Religious beliefs 30.
Religious differences 28.
Religious energy 48.
Religious persecution 166.
Remain nebulous 23.
Reputation of being tough 104.
Resentment toward men 90.
Respect and love 96.
Respond to it with honesty 27.
Restaurant entrepreneurs 82.
Restricting of guns 43.
Returning home 57.
Reward with money 65.
Righteous indignation 85.
Rigid stances 136.
Road rage 29.
Roberts, Cokie 43.
Robinson, Tom 140.
Root cause 39,73.
Rooted in good 122.
Rose, Charlie 42.
Russell, Steven 34.

Sadistic 39.
Safe relationship 53.
Sake of enhancement 149.
Scale of importance 61,63.
School administrators 165.

School power structures 103.
"second sex" 91.
Secondary relationships 113.
Seductive addictions 8.
Seductive illusion 151.
Segregation 100.
Self-betrayal 3.
Self-destruction 31.
Self-dignity 4.
Self-employment 59.
Self-examination 109,126.
Self-indulgence 112.
Self-indulgent 50.
Self-inflicted wounds 10.
Self-loathing 89,94.
Self-perception 2,21.
Self-redemption 67.
Self-restricting 147.
Self-righteous 147.
Selfish and self-centered 97.
Semblance of cohesiveness 143.
Sense of community 32,112.
Sense of victimization 119.
Sensible solutions 40.
Sensitivity 15.
Sexism 27.
Sexual domination 35.
Sexual vulnerability 91.
Shame and indignity. 115.
Shame-based behavior 115, 117,119.
Shout louder 41.
Side of town 21.
Simulated shooting drill 164.
Sins of the father and mother 136.

What We Are

Sixteen years old 88.
Slander and gossip 162.
Slavery 140.
Small business entrepreneur 60.
Social change 145.
Social cover 13,50,152.
Social development 20.
Socially acceptable 13.
Socially dependent 45.
Societal crisis 41.
"somebodyness" 111.
Something less than good 22,37.
Something other than good 9,14,18,74, 84,86, 89,93, 95,99,109,134,162.
Something other than good and bad 136.
Something other than good, bad, or evil 15,16,39, 45, 49,50, 73,108,114, 116, 120.
Something other than good, bad, or evil. 121,124,138, 147,159,160,162,166.
Something other than good or bad 52,98,154.
Spiral downward 71,83, 117.
Spirit of this woman 82.
Spiritual development 48.
Spiritual domination 35.
Spiritual grounding 151.
Spiritual pathway's 158.
Spiritual skills 21.
Spiritual success 56.
Spiritual transition 110.
Spiritually wounded 97.
Sports 91.
Standards for behavior 56.
Starting a love affair 149.
Stockbroker 56.
"straight party ticket." 36.
Strings and props 146.
Stumbling block 41.
Style of writing 113.
Success and prosperity 65.
Suggestions for improvement 141.
Summer of 1976 133.
Superb at his craft 90.
Supporting and encouraging 163.
Surprise and encouragement 131.
Sustain and preserve life 20.
Sweeping generalizations 64,159.
Symptoms of a problem 72.

Take a vacation 15.
Talk shows 42.
Tax laws 60.
Teacher 70.
Team success 58.
Technological life 22.
Temporary forgetfulness 3.
"the apple does not fall far from the tree." 30.
The equation 10.
"the more things change, 45.
The Oregonian 32.

Who We Are

The Seattle Times 26.
"this bad apple will be dealt with justly." 101.
Thoughts and feelings 131.
Three-year drunk 93.
Too revealing 131.
Total disappointment 104.
Trained specialist 14,15.
Transform my manuscript 129.
Trend-setters 75.
Trustworthy 53.
Twenty-first century 22,67,74.

Ultimate freedom 75.
Unbelievably depressed 132.
Unconscionable cruelty 61.
Unconscious level 128.
Undeniable good 135.
Undeniable truth 124.
Undeniably good 1,5,16, 46, 50,153.
Unethical and corrupt 19.
Unethical behavior 108.
Unhealthy agenda 13.
Uninspired writings 157.
Unitarian 157.
United States of America 74.
Universal truth 125.
University of Chicago 93.
University of Washington 95.
Unmistakably sound and good 116,119.
Unnecessary suffering 66.
Untimely death 116.

Unworthy and bad 95.
Unworthy and undeserving 134.
Upperclassmen 100.
Use against me 131.
Usurps the dignity 145.

Validated and approved of 133.
Vast and worldly experiences 35.
Verbal attacks 42.
Viable solution 72.
Victim of racism 165.
Victimize 37.
Victims 73.
Violence 68,117,161.
Violent behavior 153.

Washington, Seattle 95.
Way of life 51.
"We do not write in order to be 126.
Wealth of unbiased dialog 41.
Weaponry and his Bible 155.
Weapons of domination 137.
Well-being 108.
Western civilization 155.
What 47,49,55,57,65,87,89, 122,124,147,148,154, 161,166.
What I am 4.
What I was 12.
What you are world 151.
White House 52.
White students 104.
White supremacist 166.

185

What We Are

Whites and blacks 137.
Who 46,48,49,51,54, 55,57, 58,65,68 ,71,74,75,84, 86 ,89,94,97,104,113, 11 8,122,136,144,146, 148,150,152,154,161.
Who I am 4,16.
Who I was 12.
Widespread lawlessness 43.
Will, George 43.
Williams, Brian 42.
Willing to show up 68.
Win at all costs 31.
Wisconsin, Williams Bay 164.
With my chest out 131.
Women and minorities 141.
Women to accept one another 137.
Workday 57.
Working-class 59.
Workplace 61, 65.
World community 126.
World of magic and illusion 146.
World Series 61.
World War II 111.
Would-be villains 164.
Writing experiences 127.
Writings of the Bible 158.

Young America 155.